Do-It-Yourself

TRUMPET

BY MATT LUDWIG

To access audio and video visit:
www.halleonard.com/mylibrary

Enter Code
1205-9413-9211-3365

ISBN 978-1-70512-693-6

Visit Hal Leonard Online at
www.halleonard.com

World headquarters, contact:
Hal Leonard
7777 West Bluemound Road
Milwaukee, WI 53213
Email: info@halleonard.com

In Europe, contact:
Hal Leonard Europe Limited
1 Red Place
London, W1K 6PL
Email: info@halleonardeurope.com

In Australia, contact:
Hal Leonard Australia Pty. Ltd.
4 Lentara Court
Cheltenham, Victoria, 3192 Australia
Email: info@halleonard.com.au

CONTENTS

SONG INDEX

INTRODUCTION

Congratulations and welcome to the wonderful community of trumpet players! You have joined the ranks of some incredible musicians including such amazing performers as Wynton Marsalis, Arturo Sandoval, Maynard Ferguson, Ingrid Jensen, Allen Vizzutti, Alison Balsom, Herb Alpert, Louis Armstrong, Miles Davis, Doc Severinsen and many others. The trumpet has a rich and varied history, one that is steeped in tradition and innovation. The trumpet is an amazingly versatile instrument that is equally at home in the classical music hall, jazz club, blues band, and rock band. Once you get started, you will find great joy in playing some of the most iconic songs ever written—played only as a trumpet can. Let's get started!

You will be taken step-by-step through the process of learning a new instrument: from assembling the trumpet to reading notes, and finally playing songs that you have heard on the radio, in movies, and on television. It may be tempting to jump around the book to play your favorite pieces, but each page progresses forward by building on the previous songs and lessons.

There are parts of over 150 songs that reinforce topics covered throughout this book. Whether your favorite genre is rock, pop, jazz, classical, country, rap, R&B, musical and movie soundtracks, traditional bugle calls, or others, there are many songs that you'll recognize and enjoy learning to play. In addition to exercises, there are "Toolboxes" throughout this book that introduce new concepts as you go. Enjoy the journey and welcome to the trumpet club!

On page 1, you will find a unique code. Go to **www.halleonard.com/mylibrary** and enter that code to give access to audio and video online, for download or streaming. There you will find expert video instruction to get you started on the right foot, plus video and audio demonstration of many songs found in this book. These spots are indicated throughout the book by these symbols:

This book also includes PLAYBACK+, a multi-functional audio player that allows you to slow down audio without changing pitch, set loop points, and pan left or right—available exclusively from Hal Leonard.

LESSON 1:
Assembly and Instrument Care

PARTS OF THE TRUMPET

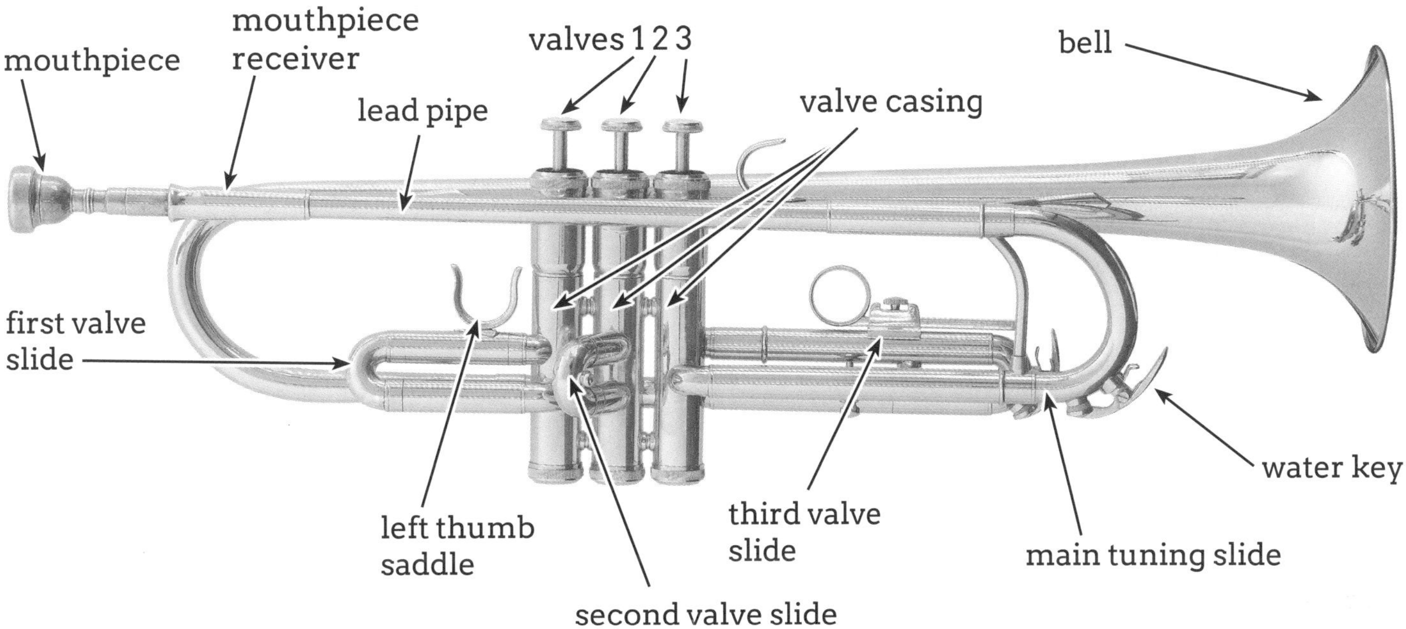

The trumpet is a surprisingly simple instrument of approximately five feet of brass piping and a mouthpiece. For the most part, daily maintenance is quite simple, but it is important to keep the trumpet looking and playing like new.

OPENING THE TRUMPET CASE

When you first open a trumpet case, the mouthpiece should be in its slot and the trumpet will be totally assembled, with all the slides pushed in. Make sure you open the case with the latches pointing down, so the case opens up and away from you. If you fail to do this, you will have the unfortunate experience of your trumpet crashing to the floor.

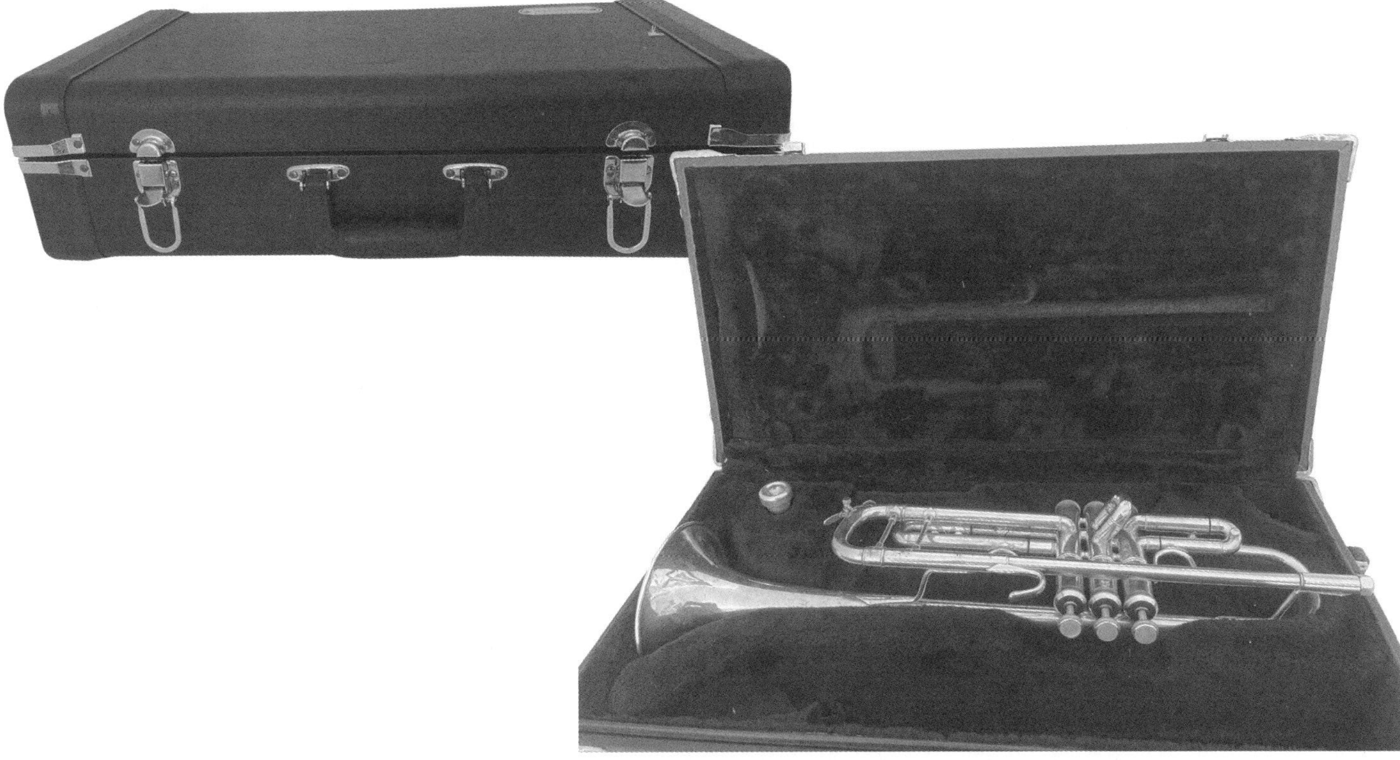

TRUMPET HAND POSITION

Here's the recommended procedure for getting the trumpet ready to play:

LEFT HAND:

1. Pick up the trumpet by lifting it around the valve casing, and hold with your left hand as shown.
2. Make sure that you have a good, solid grip, but not too tight. The left hand should support the weight of the trumpet.
3. For most players, the ring finger should slide through the third valve slide. In later lessons, we will discuss moving the third valve slide in and out to assist with tuning. If your hand is too large for your ring finger to fit through the ring, you can set it just outside the ring.
4. If your trumpet has a first valve trigger present, your thumb should rest on it with the pad of your thumb.

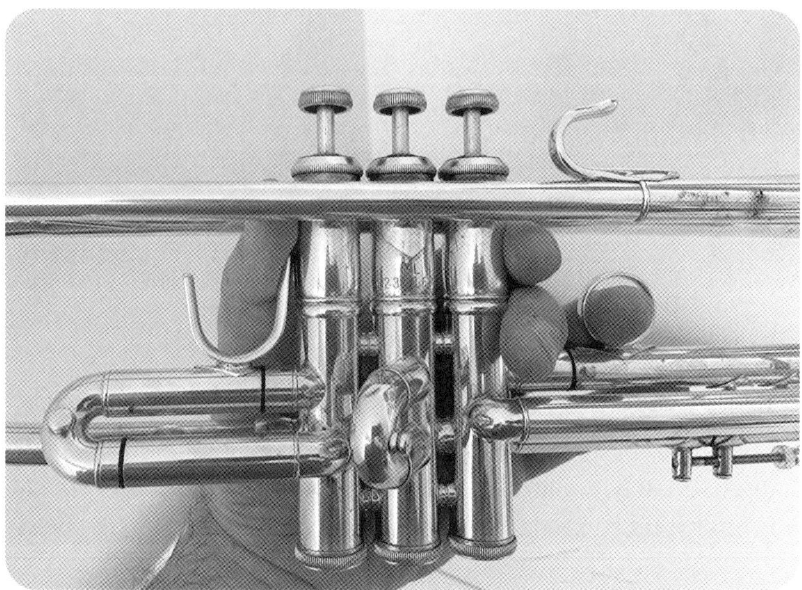

LEFT HAND

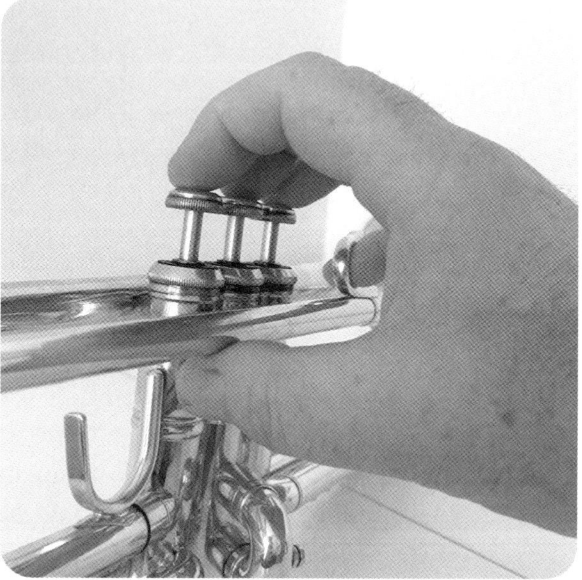

RIGHT HAND

RIGHT HAND:

1. Rest the right hand with the fleshy part of the side of the thumb under the lead pipe just in front of the first valve. Your pinky should rest just inside the pinky ring.
2. Curl your index, middle, and ring fingers over the valves. IMPORTANT: it's good to get into the habit of maintaining curled fingers and using the fleshy part of your fingertips to press down the valves. Try to avoid "flat finger" syndrome, and use the end of your fingers to push the valves down. Many players fall into this bad habit, and it will lead to problems later. Valves should be pressed as straight down as possible.
3. If held properly, the right hand should support no weight of the instrument, so it is free to manipulate the valves. The pinky ring should only be used as a guide. Many players choose to set their pinky outside the pinky ring to increase their flexibility and speed on the valves.

ASSEMBLY AND INSTRUMENT CARE

The recommended procedure for getting the trumpet ready to play is as follows:

1. After picking up the trumpet and holding it solidly with the left hand, insert the mouthpiece into the lead pipe with your right hand and gently twist clockwise with a bit of downward pressure until the mouthpiece locks into position.
2. Pull the tuning slide out about ½". (This will be adjusted when tuning later.)

Lubricate the valves. 

Unscrew each valve and pull the valves out about halfway as shown without twisting them. Put about three or four drops of valve oil on the surface of the valve. Before placing the valves back into the valve casing, look to be sure the plastic valve guide lines up with a notch in the valve casing. (See images below.) When the valves and the casing are aligned, place the valve back into the trumpet and screw in the valve tops. IMPORTANT: do not twist the valves in a circular motion to distribute the oil because circular micro-ridges may form on the valve surface and may reduce valve action. Also, it is important to use only valve oil, not any other type of household oil products. Valve oil is available from nearly all music retailers.

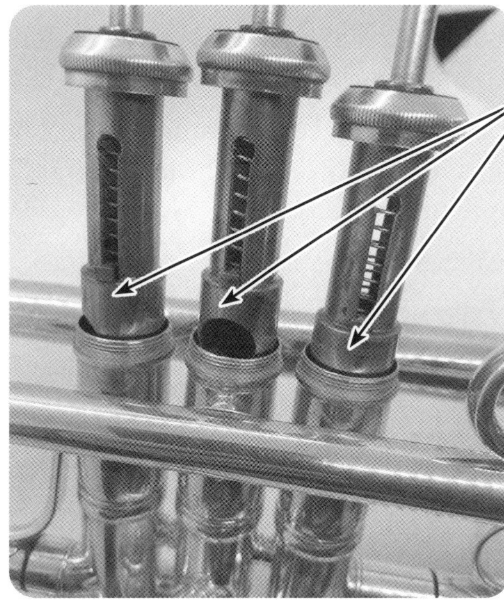

Valve oil goes on this part of the valves.

If you feel an air blockage when playing, it is likely due to a valve that is misaligned. Another possibility is that the valves got mixed up, impeding air flow. Each valve is marked with a 1, 2, or 3, usually somewhere on the stem. Make sure each valve is in the proper order and aligned within the casing.

Empty the water key. 

You will need to blow through the instrument to get the water out; make sure you blow, not buzz. Throughout your playing session, you will have to empty the water out of your water key located on the main tuning slide. Some trumpets also have water keys on the third valve slide, while others do not. It is recommended that you empty the condensation on an absorbent pad or towel, rather than directly on the floor or carpet. If you still hear a gurgling sound, it means that water is trapped somewhere in the instrument, and you may need to disassemble more pipes to get it out.

When finished playing, the following is recommended:

1. Remove mouthpiece by twisting it counterclockwise and lifting up.
2. Push the tuning slide (and any other slides that may be out a bit) all the way back in. This is important to avoid oxidation of the metal.
3. Wipe down the entire trumpet with a dry, soft cloth rag.
4. Close the case, set the latches, and you're ready to go for next time.

LONG-TERM INSTRUMENT CARE

Weekly Maintenance:

1. Grease all slides: First, disassemble the tuning slide and second valve slide and place them on a lint-free towel. Apply a small amount of slide grease (available at most music supply stores) to each pipe and re-insert. For the first and third valve slides, it is recommended that you use trombone slide cream or a lighter grease, since these slides are designed to be moved in and out and require a grease that is lighter than the grease on the tuning slide and second valve slide.
2. Clean the mouthpiece. You will need to purchase a mouthpiece cleaning brush from a music retailer. It is recommended that you clean the mouthpiece under lukewarm water without any soap.

Bi-Monthly Maintenance:

Give your trumpet a bath!

1. Take the trumpet apart and soak all pieces except the valves in a bathtub or plastic laundry tub with lukewarm water (not hot water, since hot water can damage the finish). If desired, just a small dab of dish detergent can be used.
2. Scrub out all slides (not the valves) with a cleaning snake (not the mouthpiece brush). This can be purchased as part of a trumpet cleaning kit.
3. Run the valves under lukewarm running water, being careful not to get the felt at the top of the valves wet, and at the same time snake out the inner part of the valves with a valve cleaning brush (also available as part of a trumpet cleaning kit).
4. Rinse out all parts of the trumpet to remove any remaining residue.
5. Towel dry all parts of the trumpet.
6. Once all parts are dry, oil the valves and grease all the slides.

LESSON 2:
Understanding Music

The better a person gets at learning the language of music, the more fun playing can be! Music is broken down into the basic elements of reading notes, rhythms, dynamics (how loud or soft the music should be) and articulations (how hard or soft to tongue the notes). We'll talk about notes and rhythms now and talk about articulations and dynamics later in the book.

This lesson, along with Lesson 3, is an overview of reading music. You are encouraged to reference these pages as you encounter the concepts throughout the book

Music is a language that you can read and write. Like any language, music has its own symbols and structure. You learned your native language because you were surrounded by it from birth. If you surround yourself with the language of music, you will become familiar with it over time.

THE STAFF

Music is organized on a staff of five horizontal lines. It is capable of displaying virtually all there is to know about a piece of music. Two important things it shows us is how music moves over space and time (rhythm) and how high or low the notes are (pitch).

Rhythm is organized horizontally along the staff and will be covered in the next lesson. Pitch is organized vertically using the lines and spaces; the higher a note's placement, the higher the pitch.

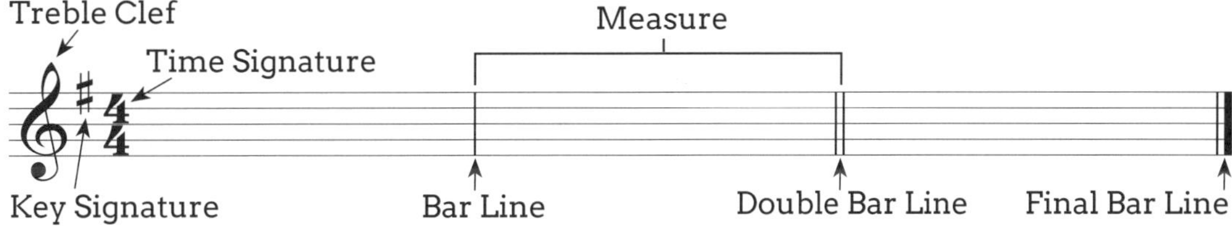

Treble Clef

The treble clef establishes the second line as the note G. The symbol itself is an ornate G, also known as a G Clef. Notice that it curls around the second line to establish G. There are other clefs, but the trumpet only reads in treble clef.

Bar Lines

Bar lines divide the staff into measures. A double bar line is used to mark something significant that occurs in the music, such as a new section. The final bar line is used to mark the end of the song.

Measures

A measure is the space between bar lines. It's also known as a "bar." The movement of music (rhythm) is established from left to right through this space.

Time Signature

The time signature determines how many beats are in each measure and what type of note receives one beat. This is covered in Lesson 3.

Key Signature

The key signature assigns either sharps or flats (never both together) for particular notes for the duration of the song. This is covered later in this lesson as well as in Lesson 6.

Spaces

Notes in the spaces in ascending order happen to spell the word FACE.

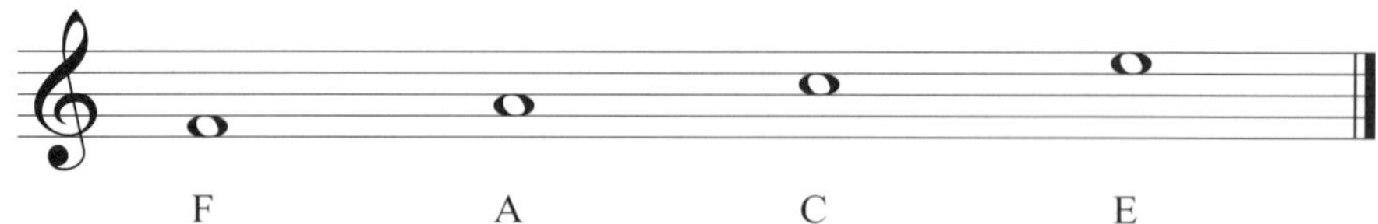

Lines

An acronym commonly used to remember notes on the lines in ascending order is Every Good Boy Does Fine.

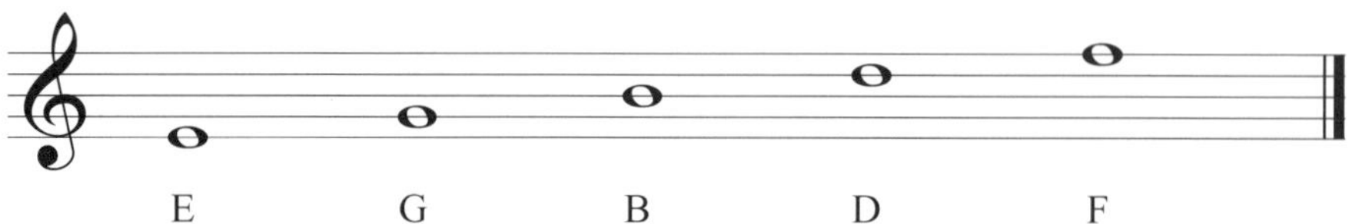

Alphabet

When the spaces and lines are combined, you'll see that music ascends alphabetically from A to G. You may find it helpful to memorize and locate A as you learn.

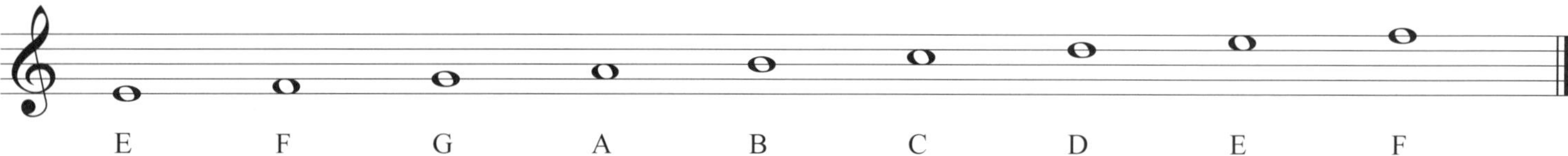

Ledger Lines

The staff can be thought of as an infinite number of lines; five of them are visible and the rest are invisible. When a note is needed above or below the staff, small lengths of line become visible. For instance, high B is in the space above the first ledger line. Low C is on the first ledger line below the staff.

Notice that this is a continuation of the alphabet.

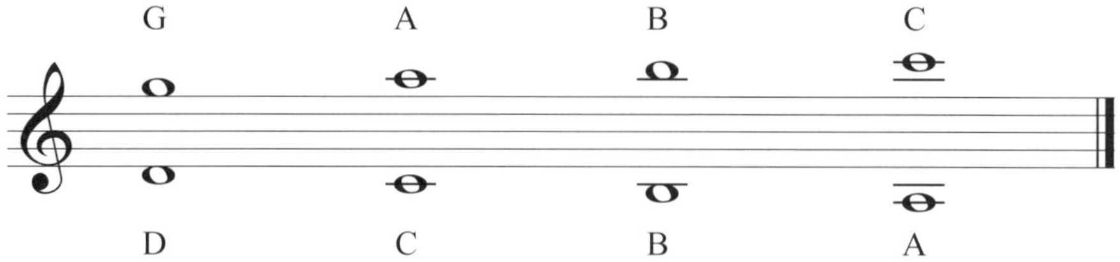

Accidentals

A half-step is the smallest interval (distance) between two notes. A note is altered by one half-step the following three ways:

An accidental applies to a note for one measure. In this example the last note does not require a natural to cancel the flat; this is accomplished by the key signature.

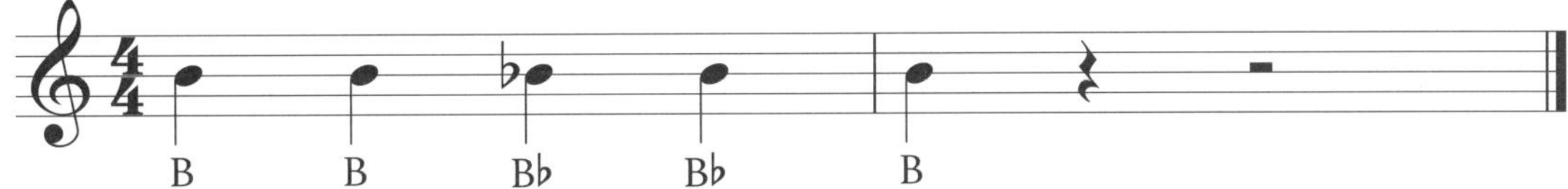

Sometimes you'll see a courtesy reminder in parentheses. This example will sound the same as the previous example.

Here are two examples of accidentals in the context of a key signature. The key signature assigns sharps to all F's and C's. The natural symbol cancels each one until the next measure. Notice there is no courtesy reminder in the second measure.

LESSON 3:
Understanding Rhythm

TIME SIGNATURES

Rhythm is based on evenly spaced pulses that we call beats. The distribution of beats is determined by the time signature. The top number represents how many beats are in each measure, while the bottom number represents what kind of note receives one beat.

There are 4 beats per measure
A quarter note ♩ is one beat

There are 6 beats per measure
An eighth note ♪ is one beat

NOTE AND REST DURATIONS

The most common time signature is 4/4 time. The bottom number in 4/4 determines the following durations, whether sound (notes) or silence (rests):

WHOLE NOTE & REST
Each is four beats

HALF NOTE & REST
Each is two beats and
one half of a whole note

QUARTER NOTE & REST
Each is one beat and
one quarter of a whole note

EIGHTH NOTE & REST
Each is 1/2 beat and
one eighth of a whole note

SIXTEENTH NOTE & REST
Each is 1/4 beat and
one sixteenth of a whole note

BEAMS

Eighth notes and sixteenth notes are joined by horizontal beams, typically in groups of two and four. Eighth notes can be joined together with sixteenth notes, as you'll see in Lesson 14.

COUNTING METHOD

In this book, we will count rhythm using the method shown in the chart below. Note durations from the previous section have been placed into a table with sixteen columns. This table is always theoretically present in a musician's thinking when playing in 4/4 time. It represents all the ways notes and beats can be divided into smaller parts.

SUBDIVIDING

Subdivide notes in order to keep your place and play with rhythmic accuracy. This is done by thinking internally, tapping a foot, or using a metronome. (For information about metronomes, see page 33.) You can do this right now: whistle, hum, or simply exhale while tapping your foot and counting in your head (stop on 5). You just performed a whole note.

Another example of subdividing that you can do right now: clap four quarter notes while counting eighth notes: "1-&-2-&-3-&-4-&" (& = and). You'll say a number on each clap with &'s between claps. We call the numbers downbeats, and the &'s upbeats.

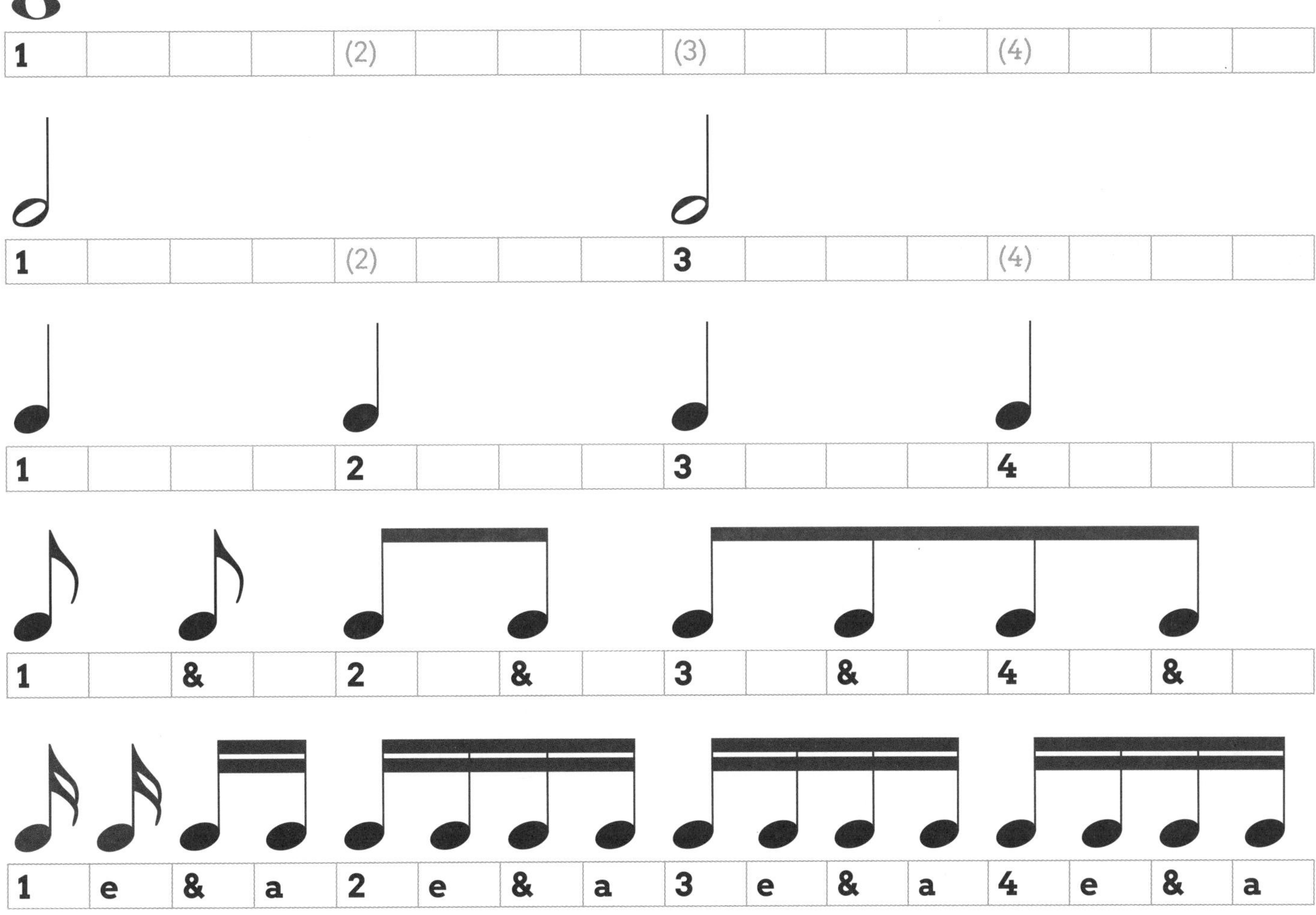

RESTS

Rests are counted and subdivided just like notes but are silent. Some rests are added here with the counting italicized in parentheses.

Try counting the half note in the second line like this: while clapping the downbeats, say a long "one" and stop on the third clap.

TIES

A tie is an arc that joins two notes of the same pitch together. In this example, two quarter notes are tied and become a single note worth two beats. Ties are not to be confused with slurs which use the same symbol, but connects notes of different pitches. Slurs will be covered in Lesson 9.

ADDITION

As you saw with ties, rhythm involves a little math. Notice beat four of the sixteenth note line (bottom right of the table). There is an eighth rest instead of two sixteenth rests because it is more efficient: 1/4 𝄿 + 1/4 𝄿 = 1/2 𝄾

Another bit of math we do involves dotted rhythms. This is covered on page 25.

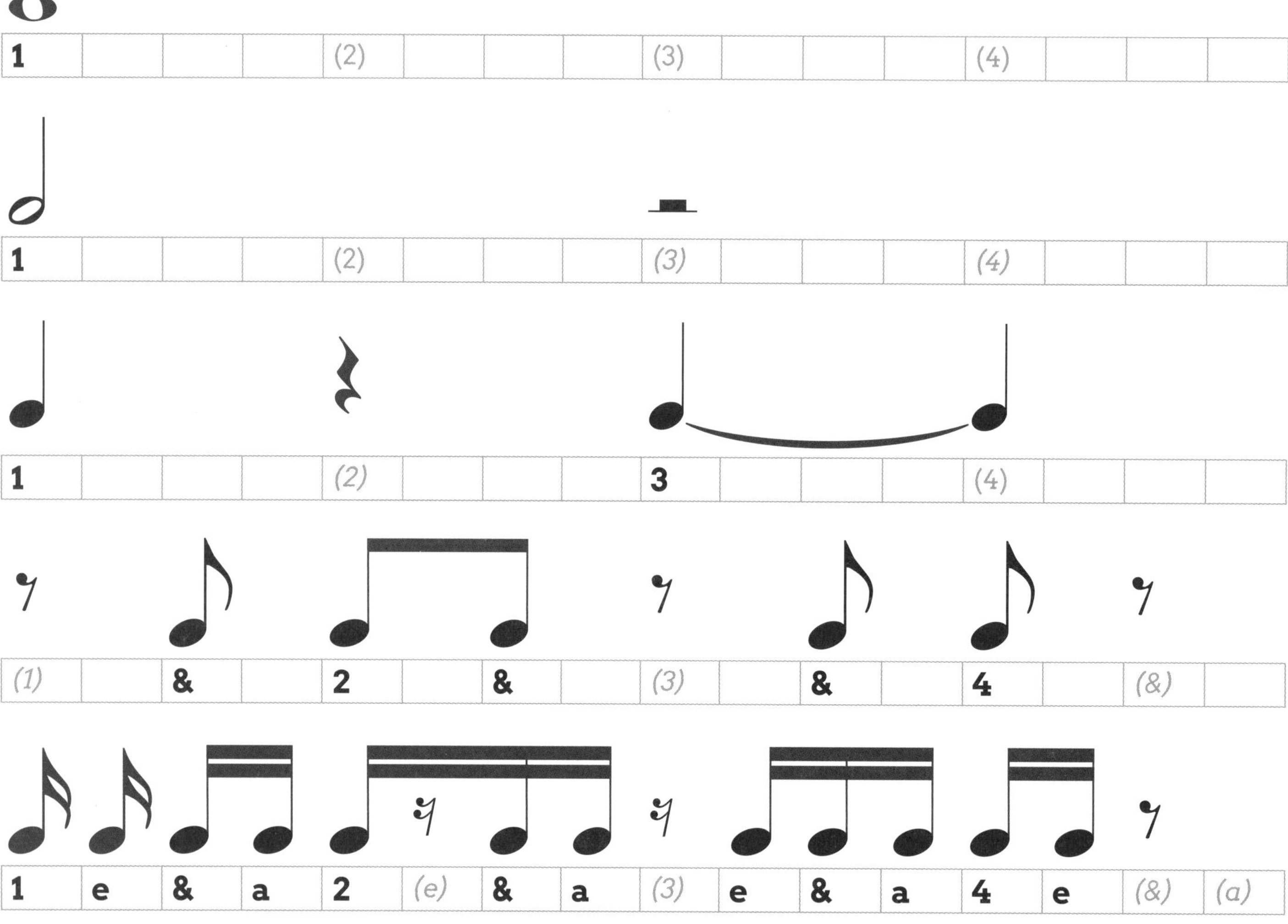

LESSON 4:
Lip Buzzing

Like the foundation of a well-built house, the ability to buzz on a mouthpiece is one of the most important skills in trumpet playing. How does one do that well?

First, we must make sure your lips are in the correct position to make the best "buzz."

BUZZING WITHOUT THE MOUTHPIECE

Say the letter "M" but do it slowly by saying "eemmmm" and hold it for at least 10 seconds. Place your fingers up to the corner of your lips and press. Do you feel what your muscles are doing? If you're doing this correctly, the corners of your lips should be tight.

Next, look in the mirror and say "eemmmm" once again. You should notice that your lips curl in a bit, and there is very little to no red part of your lip showing. Feel the corners of your lips and make sure they are tight. If not, try to make the "eemmmm" sound and see if you can make the corners tighter.

Then, while looking in the mirror, say "emmmm – phfft" and try to make your lips vibrate while holding the corners in. You may notice when looking in the mirror that some red part of your lips starts to show. That's okay as long as it's not too much. If you're only able to say "eemmm – phfft," but your corners are no longer taught, try to figure out how to do it and keep the corners tight.

BUZZING WITH THE MOUTHPIECE

Now it is time to start working with the mouthpiece!

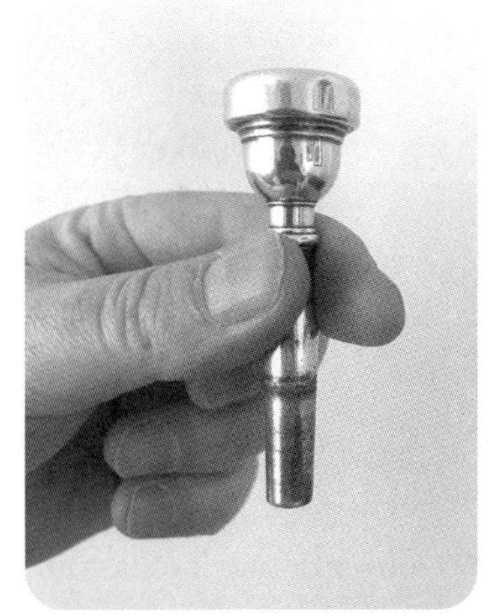

Start by grasping the mouthpiece in your left hand by holding it as shown between your thumb and index finger and slowly bring it up to your lips. Do this very slowly the first few times so you can get a sense of where the mouthpiece meets your lips.

Next, position the mouthpiece so that an equal amount of top lip and bottom lip is in the mouthpiece. This is important to get right the first few times, and I would encourage you to use a mirror to see where you are setting up with your lips.

Then, repeat the buzzing exercises that you did without the mouthpiece, but now with the mouthpiece, being careful not to push the mouthpiece into your lips too much with your left hand. Spend a few moments getting used to this, check your lip corners for tightness, and make sure that not much of the red part of your lips is showing when you buzz. The position of your mouth on the mouthpiece is called your **embouchure**.

When you first start buzzing, you may notice that your lips get tired. If this happens, stop for a moment and rest. When you feel comfortable buzzing on the mouthpiece and can create different pitches, you are ready to try playing on the trumpet!

LESSON 5:
Long Tone Exercises

After buzzing on the mouthpiece, you are now ready to begin making sounds on the trumpet!

Long tones are useful for gaining strength and flexibility in your lips and are often used to warm up the muscles. When taking a breath, the throat should be open, much like a yawn. Also, it is helpful to keep space between the top and bottom teeth. Keep your shoulders relaxed and focus on the chest cavity expanding out while silently taking a breath. **Always begin each note by *tonguing* (moving your tongue as if you were saying "tee." Avoid saying or making a "th" sound like "tha").**

TOOLBOX

Toolbox Tip: Fingering Diagrams
We will introduce notes by using a graphical system for showing fingerings for various notes.

"1" is the first valve (closest to the player) and will be notated by the left-most circle. "2" is the second valve and will be notated by the center circle. "3" is the third valve (furthest from the player) and will be notated by the right-most circle. An empty circle indicates the valve is up and a dark circle indicates the valve is pressed down.

Example: ○○○ All valves open (up) ●●● All valves closed (down)

Play a G and hold it. It should be played with no valves down (open). Be sure to count to four. Repeat this exercise several times to get used to tonguing and counting.

NEW NOTE: G

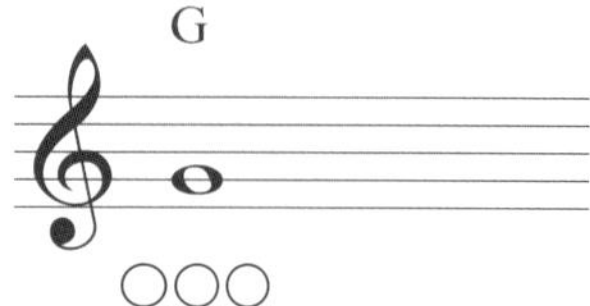

NEW NOTES: F, E, D, and C

Now you are ready to play descending long tones and get used to playing some other notes. Let's introduce F, E, D, and C.

- ❜ A **breath mark** tells you where to breathe in a piece of music.

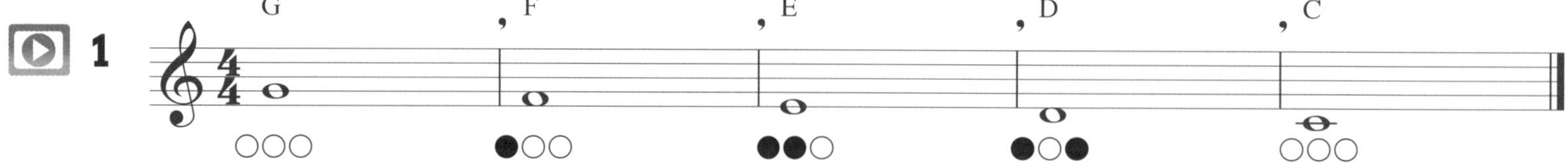

Using the notes that you have just learned, try this note interval exercise. Be sure you hold each whole note and whole rest for four counts each. During the four-count rest, take a good breath. When you play "C," it is fingered the same as the "G," but your lips will be more relaxed and buzz slower on the "C."

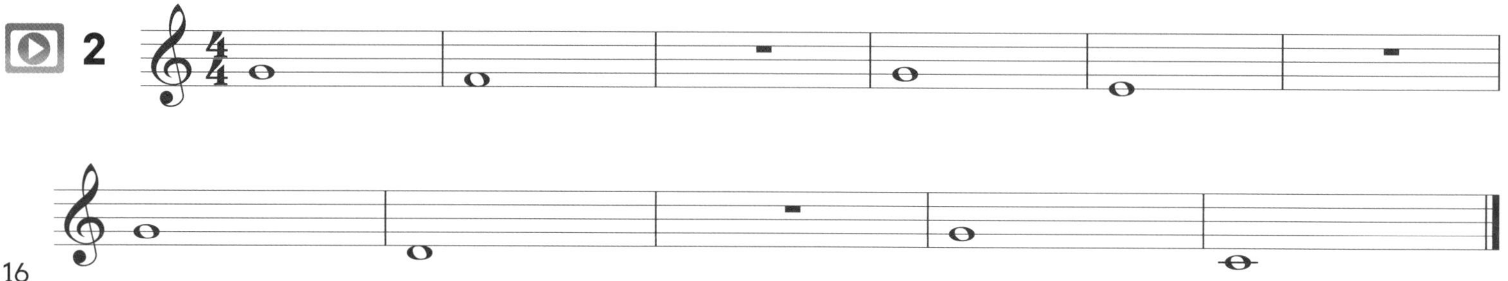

Breathe as necessary.

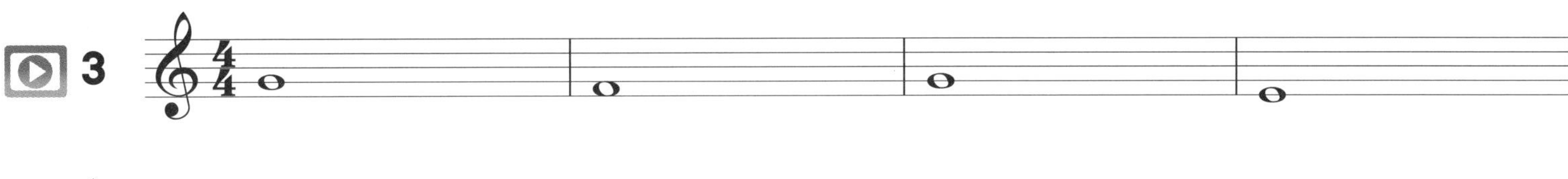

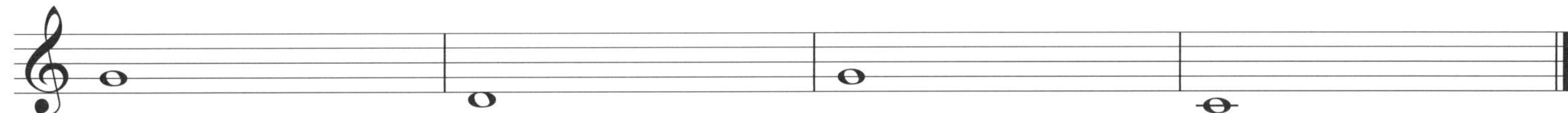

Half Note 

A **half note** receives two counts (or beats) of sound in 4/4 time.

Half Rest

A **half rest** receives two counts (or beats) of silence in 4/4 time.

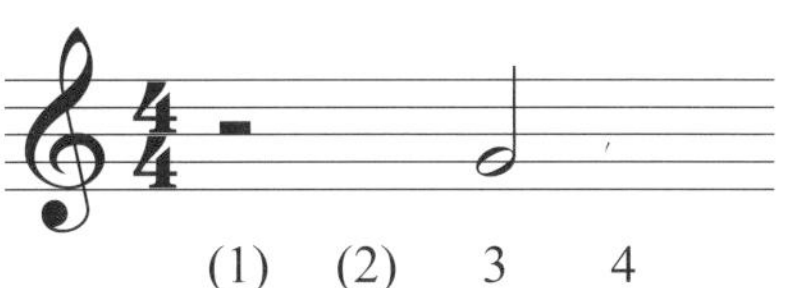

Play each note for two counts. Notice that the rests are also two counts.

Always start your buzz by moving your tongue as if you were saying “tee.”

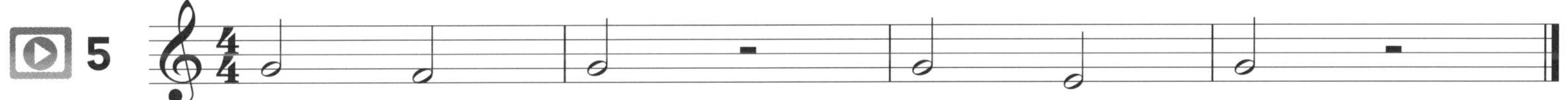

Repeat the same instructions as the previous exercise.

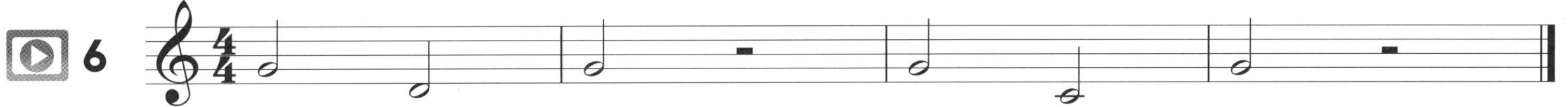

Combine whole notes and half notes to complete this exercise.

LESSON 6:
Playing Higher

You can make your trumpet sound higher by tightening your embouchure and allowing the aperture (the hole your lips create) to get smaller. Also, to play higher it helps to think about buzzing your lips faster and using "cool" (faster) air instead of "warm" (slower) air.

Subdivision

Breaking the beat into smaller, even pieces, rather than just counting the strong beats.

Example: 1 <u>&</u> 2 <u>&</u> 3 <u>&</u> 4 <u>&</u>

NEW NOTES:

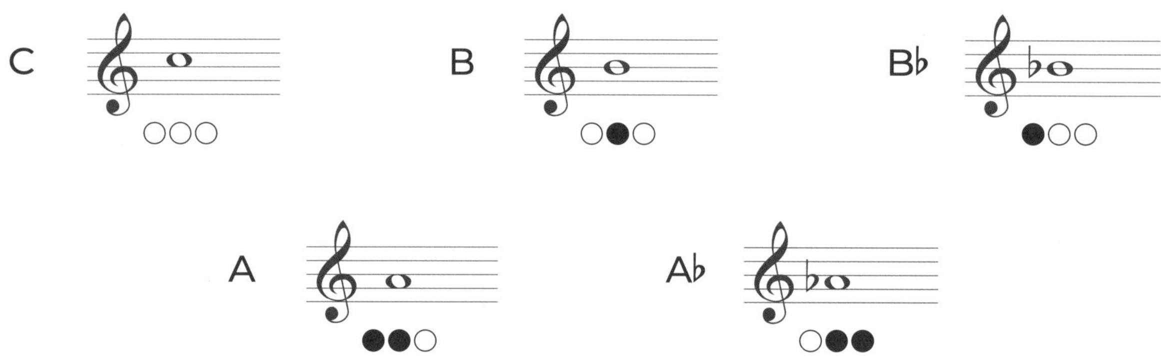

NEW NOTE: C

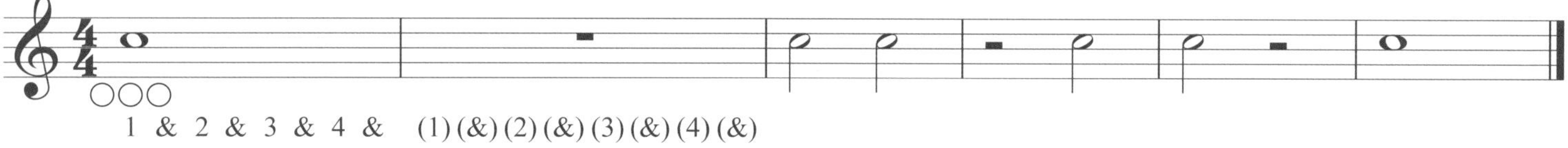

Remember to always start each note with your tongue!

If necessary, check pitches with a tuner. The standard trumpet sounds one note lower than it is written, so a C will show as a B♭ on a tuner or tuner app.

NEW NOTE: B

NEW NOTE: B♭

NEW NOTE: A

NEW NOTE: A♭

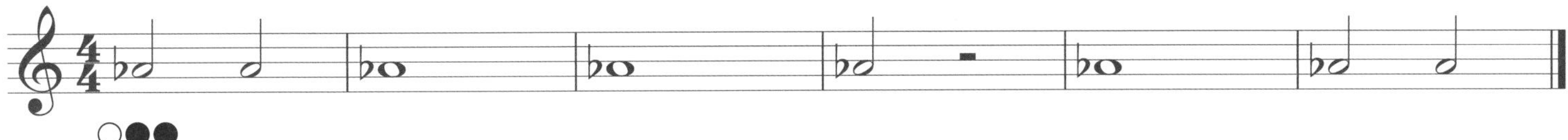

MIX 'EM UP

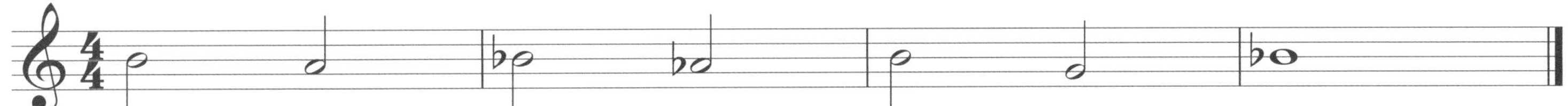

UP & DOWN

MIDDLING AROUND

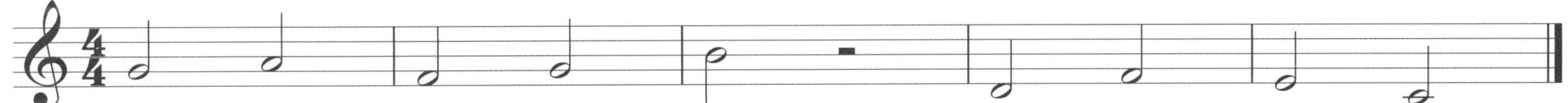

THE BELL TOWER

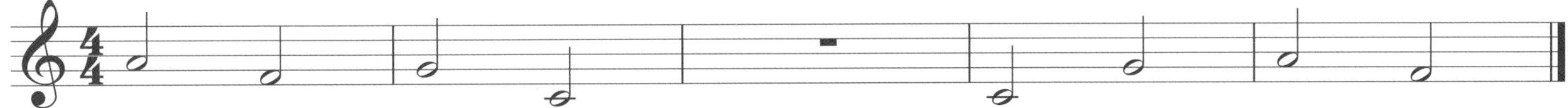

RAIN, RAIN GO AWAY

Traditional

TRUMPET VOLUNTARY

By Jeremiah Clarke

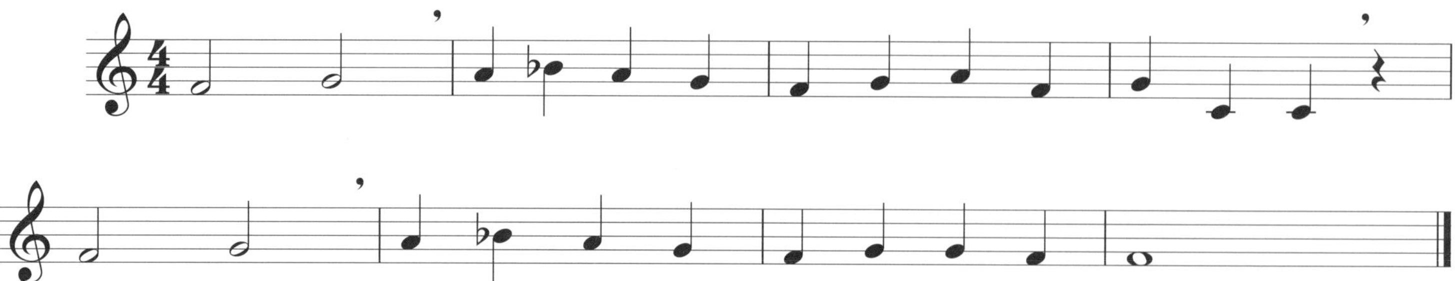

LOVE ME TENDER

Words and Music by Elvis Presley and Vera Matson

MERRILY WE ROLL ALONG

Traditional

Key Signature: Key of F Major

This key signature has one flat: B♭

A **key signature** indicates whether to play the note sharp, flat, or natural for the entire song. Flat (♭) or sharp (♯) signs are placed after the clef.

The line or space that the sharp or flat occupies indicates which notes are changed.

TOOLBOX

Toolbox Tip: Breathing
Breath marks (❜) do not always appear in music. If a song does not have a breath mark, breathe quickly when you need more air.

ODE TO JOY

from SYMPHONY NO. 9 IN D MINOR, FOURTH MOVEMENT CHORAL THEME

Words by Henry van Dyke
Music by Ludwig van Beethoven

LONDON BRIDGE

Traditional

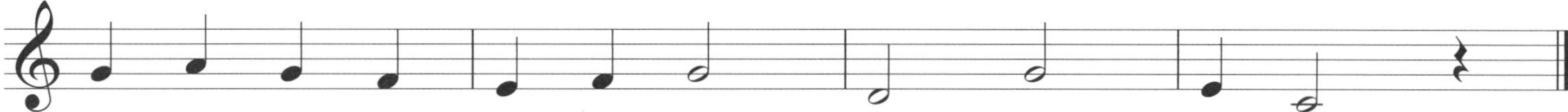

JINGLE BELLS

NOBODY KNOWS THE TROUBLE I'VE SEEN

African-American Spiritual

THE LONGEST TIME

Words and Music by Billy Joel

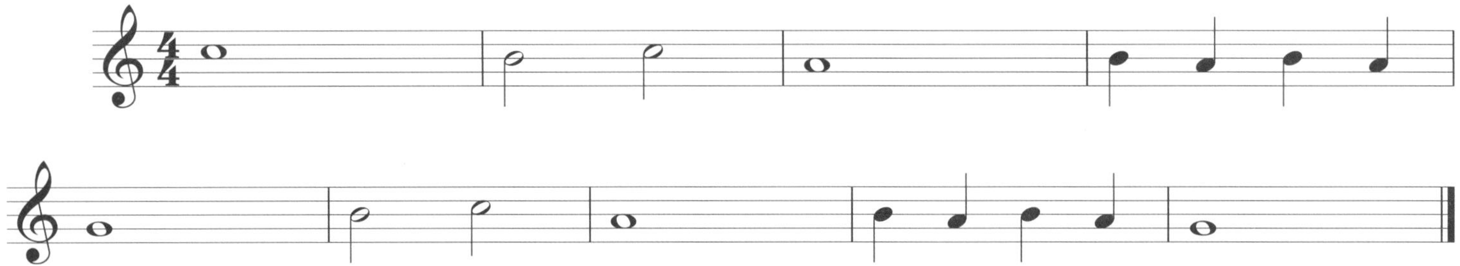

New Time Signature: 2/4

2 = 2 beats in each measure
4 = quarter note receives one beat

Eighth Note

An **eighth note** receives ½ of a beat of sound. Often, they are paired in groups of two notes.

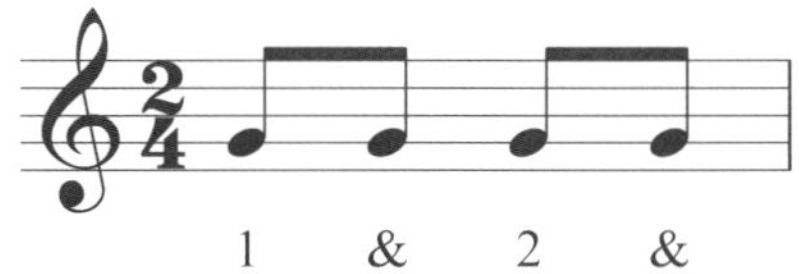

Stem Direction

Notes can have the stem pointing up or down, depending upon where they are placed in each measure. Notes above the middle line have the stems pointing down, while notes below the middle line have stems pointing up. Notes on the middle line can be written with the stems up or down.

New Note: D

FRÈRE JACQUES (ARE YOU SLEEPING?)

Traditional

LOVE STORY

Words and Music by Taylor Swift

Dynamics

Indicate how loud of soft to play the music.

Forte: loud **Piano:** soft

f ***p***

Repeat Sign

Instructs you to go back to the beginning of the music.

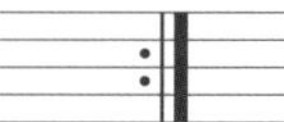

I LOVE ROCK 'N ROLL

Words and Music by Alan Merrill and Jake Hooker

WE ARE FAMILY

Words and Music by Nile Rodgers and Bernard Edwards

SHEPHERDS HEY

English Folk Song

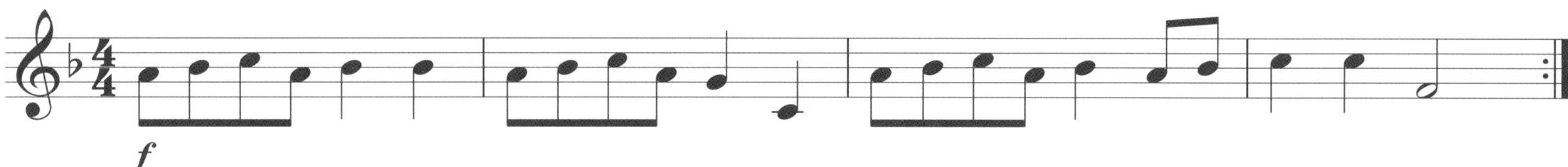

SIMPLE GIFTS

Traditional Shaker Hymn

Trumpet Talk: Tuning

The trumpet has a tuning slide (see Lesson 1 for a photo) that can be adjusted if the instrument is sharp (above pitch) or flat (below pitch). Using a tuner or smartphone app, play a third space C and look at the gauge to find out if you are in tune. If your instrument is sharp, you'll need to pull out the tuning slide. If you are flat, you'll need to push it in. **SHARP: OUT. FLAT: IN.** There are also tuning slides on the third valve (see photo) and sometimes, near the first valve. These can be used to fine-tune known problem notes on the trumpet, as explained in Lesson 16.

EVERY BREATH YOU TAKE

Music and Lyrics by Sting

More Dynamics

Mezzo forte: medium loud *mf*

Mezzo piano: medium soft *mp*

Double bar

Indicates a new section of music.

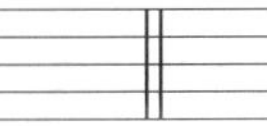

New Time Signature: 3/4

3 = 3 beats in each measure
4 = quarter note receives one beat

Tie

Connects two or more notes of the same pitch to make one longer note.

Dotted half note

A **dotted half note** receives three counts (or beats) of sound.

A **dot** adds half the value of the note before the dot. If a half note is worth two beats, the dot would add half of the value to the existing note. 2 beats + 1 beat = 3 beats

MORNING
from PEER GYNT
By Edvard Grieg

TRUE COLORS
Words and Music by Billy Steinberg and Tom Kelly

EINE KLEINE NACHTMUSIK ("SERENADE")
First Movement Excerpt
By Wolfgang Amadeus Mozart

HALLELUJAH CHORUS
(from THE MESSIAH)
By George Frideric Handel

PIANO MAN
Words and Music by Billy Joel

New Note: B

New Note: A

Tempo: the speed of the music

Moderato: a medium speed

Allegro: fast

Intonation: Pitch Accuracy
To play with good **intonation** means you have the ability to play your instrument in tune.

Trumpet Talk

Playing the trumpet can be challenging because different notes have the same valve combination. With practice, you'll develop an ear to be able to tell the difference between notes that have the same fingerings, but be patient! This is a skill that develops over time.

BLOWIN' IN THE WIND

Words and Music by Bob Dylan

Eighth Rest

An **eighth rest** receives ½ a beat of silence.

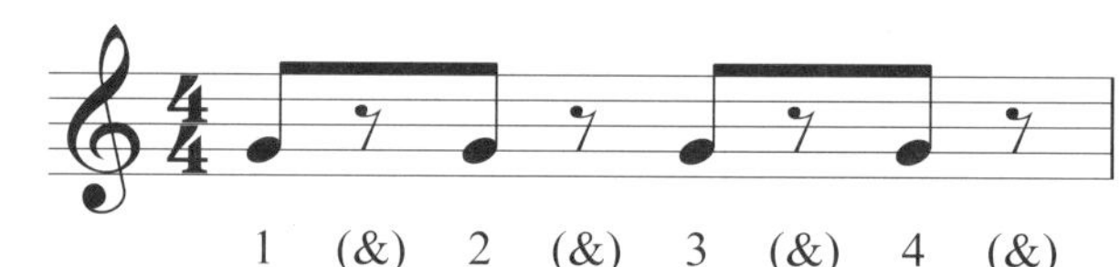

SHUT UP AND DANCE

Words and Music by Ryan McMahon, Ben Berger, Sean Waugaman, Eli Maiman, Nicholas Petricca and Kevin Ray

THE MEDALLION CALLS

from PIRATES OF THE CARIBBEAN: THE CURSE OF THE BLACK PEARL

Music by Klaus Badelt

Moderato

f

mp

Another Tempo

Andante: slower "walking" tempo (slower than moderato)

LEAN ON ME

Words and Music by Bill Withers

OPEN ARMS

Words and Music by Steve Perry and Jonathan Cain

THEME FROM "JAWS"

from the Universal Picture JAWS

By John Williams

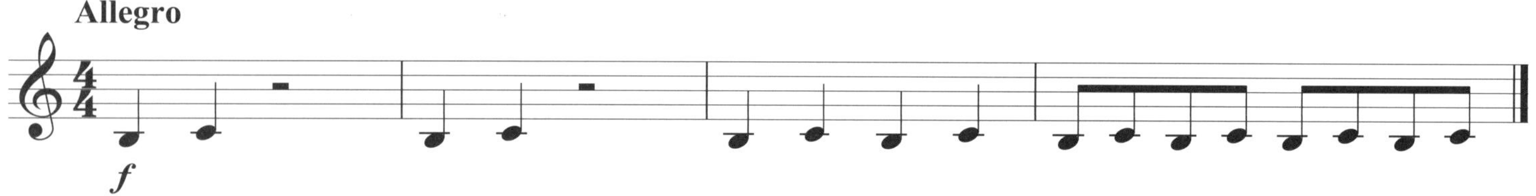

LESSON 7:
Road Maps

1st and 2nd Endings

Play through the first ending and repeat back. Play the beginning section again, but skip the first ending and continue to the second ending.

CHIAPANECAS
Mexican Folk Song

Pickup Note(s)

Pickup note(s) are a note or group of notes that occur before the first full measure of music. Sometimes a pickup note is called an anacrusis.

More Pickups

If the music has a pickup note or notes, then beats that were used in the pickup measure are often taken from the last measure of music.

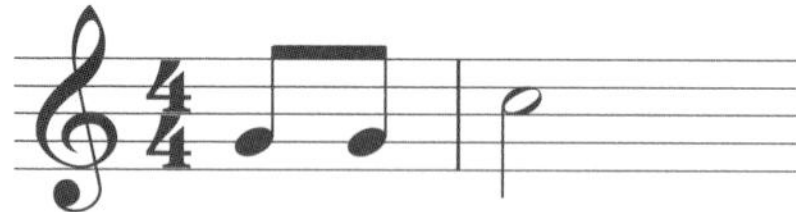

IF one beat is moved to the beginning as a pickup measure...

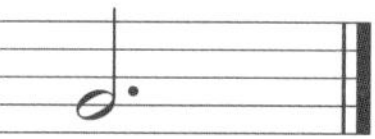

...THEN one beat is often taken from the last measure.

TOOLBOX

Toolbox Tip: Internal Repeats

Not all repeats send you back to the beginning of a song. If you find a repeat sign at the beginning of a measure, that is where you go back to on a repeat.

BAD ROMANCE

Words and Music by Stefani Germanotta and Nadir Khayat

TOOLBOX

Toolbox Tip: Metronome

A **metronome** is a device used to keep a steady tempo.

Setting a metronome to the tempo of the piece of music being practiced is key to developing good musicianship. Unless otherwise marked, music is intended to played at a constant speed throughout the piece. When a passage of music is challenging or becoming difficult, slow down the metronome to practice the notes and rhythms correctly. Once mastery of the music at a slower tempo has been achieved, gradually increase the tempo until the marked tempo is reached. Metronomes are available at most music stores, and several excellent ones can be found online or as an app, for little or no cost.

WILLIAM TELL OVERTURE

By Gioachino Rossini

CARNIVAL OF VENICE

By Julius Benedict

Dotted Quarter Note

A **dotted quarter note** is worth 1½ beats. The dot adds half the value of the note to the existing note. (1 + ½ = 1½.) Dotted quarter notes are often accompanied by a single eighth note.

Another way to write a note that is 1½ beats is to tie an eighth note with a quarter note.

Another Tempo

Largo: very slow

LARGO

from SYMPHONY NO. 9 IN E MINOR, OP. 95 ("FROM THE NEW WORLD")

By Antonin Dvorak

ACHY BREAKY HEART (DON'T TELL MY HEART)

Words and Music by Don Von Tress

MY GIRL

Words and Music by Smokey Robinson and Ronald White

MR. TAMBOURINE MAN

Words and Music by Bob Dylan

LESSON 8:
Shuffle Feel

Shuffle: a rhythmic feel where the first note in a group of two eighth notes feels twice as long as the second note. This groove is often found in pop music.

The shuffle feel is also used in many jazz pieces of music which will be explored later in this book.

ROSANNA

Words and Music by David Paich

ISN'T SHE LOVELY

Words and Music by Stevie Wonder

BOOGIE WOOGIE BUGLE BOY

from BUCK PRIVATES

Words and Music by Don Raye and Hughie Prince

EIGHT DAYS A WEEK

Words and Music by John Lennon and Paul McCartney

Interval: the distance between notes

Octave: an interval between two notes that have the same note name. Octaves are eight note names apart.

Scales: if notes are the words in music, scales are like sentences. Most music is built on a scale with a fundamental or starting note—usually the first one. Learning scales is very important to becoming a proficient musician. In some ways, it is like learning a musical language, where our ears and fingers become accustomed to patterns and sounds. In this book, we will introduce scales of some of the most common keys.

C MAJOR SCALE

The first eight notes of "Joy to the World" are a descending scale.

JOY TO THE WORLD

Words by Isaac Watts • Music by George Frideric Handel • Adapted by Lowell Mason

ALL MY LOVING

Words and Music by John Lennon and Paul McCartney

Shuffle

FIELDS OF GOLD

Music and Lyrics by Sting

New Note: B♭

New Note: E♭

B♭ MAJOR SCALE

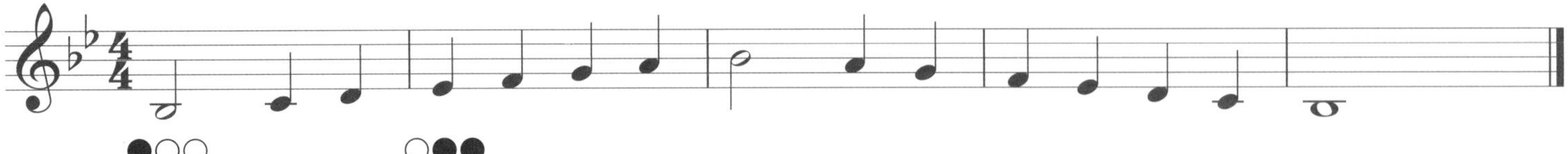

ON TOP OF OLD SMOKY

Kentucky Mountain Folksong

OH, PRETTY WOMAN

Words and Music by Roy Orbison and Bill Dees

ALLEGRO ("SPRING")

from CONCERTO IN E MAJOR "SPRING," OP. 8, NO. 1

By Antonio Vivaldi

SHE DRIVES ME CRAZY

Words and Music by David Steele and Roland Gift

STAND BY ME

(Bass Line)

Words and Music by Jerry Leiber, Mike Stoller and Ben E. King

FORREST GUMP – MAIN TITLE (FEATHER THEME)

from the Paramount Motion Picture FORREST GUMP

Music by Alan Silvestri

WHAT THE WORLD NEEDS NOW IS LOVE

Lyric by Hal David · Music by Burt Bacharach

Natural ♮

A **natural** sign cancels all previous accidentals or sharps and flats in a key signature for the rest of that measure. It is often referred to as returning a note back to its normal, or ***natural*** state.

These two notes are the same, however one is written with a natural sign because of the key signature.

Accidental

An **accidental** is a sharp, flat, or natural that appears in a measure. The note stays altered for the *rest of that measure* or until another accidental changes that note.

A courtesy accidental is a reminder that a note already exists in the key signature. It is sometimes placed in parentheses. (♮)

I'M A BELIEVER

Words and Music by Neil Diamond

TOOLBOX

Toolbox Tip: Tempo Markings

Tempos are measured by BPM, or beats per minute. When setting your metronome, consider these speeds for each tempo.

- Allegro: 120-160 BPM
- Moderato: 100-120 BPM
- Andante: 80-100 BPM
- Adagio: 60-80 BPM
- Largo: 40-60 BPM

New Tempo

Adagio: slow

JUPITER

from THE PLANETS

By Gustav Holst

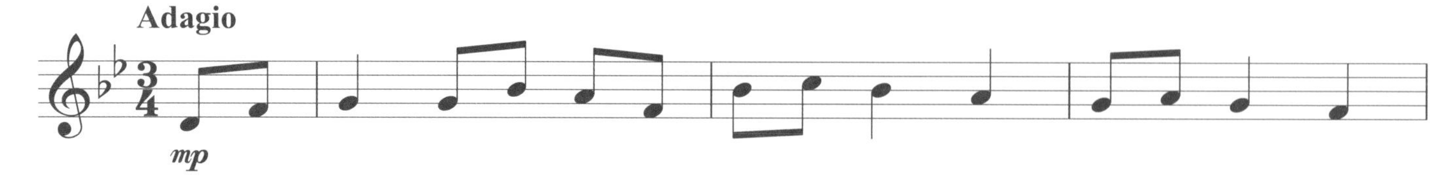

New Note: D♭

New Note: D♭

MY FAVORITE THINGS

from THE SOUND OF MUSIC

Lyrics by Oscar Hammerstein II • Music by Richard Rodgers

(SITTIN' ON) THE DOCK OF THE BAY

Words and Music by Steve Cropper and Otis Redding

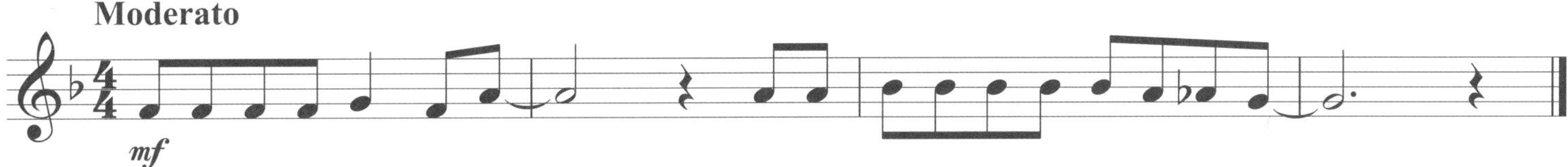

25 OR 6 TO 4

Words and Music by Robert Lamm

THEME FROM "JURASSIC PARK"

from the Universal Motion Picture JURASSIC PARK

Composed by John Williams

THE SURPRISE SYMPHONY

By Franz Joseph Haydn

WE FOUND LOVE

Words and Music by Calvin Harris

New Note: G♭

MANEATER

Words and Music by Sara Allen, Daryl Hall and John Oates

MINUET IN G

from NOTEBOOK FOR ANNA MAGDALENA BACH

By Christian Petzold

Offbeat

An **offbeat** is a beat that is not on the strong beat or a "number" in a measure. Offbeats fall between the beat in which you would tap your foot. When counting, this would generally be on the word "and."

Syncopation

When the emphasis of a beat shifts from the strong beat to the offbeat, this rhythmic change is called **syncopation**.

YOU ARE THE SUNSHINE OF MY LIFE

Words and Music by Stevie Wonder

Allegro
f
(1) (2) & 3 4 & (1) & (2) & (3) & (4) & 1

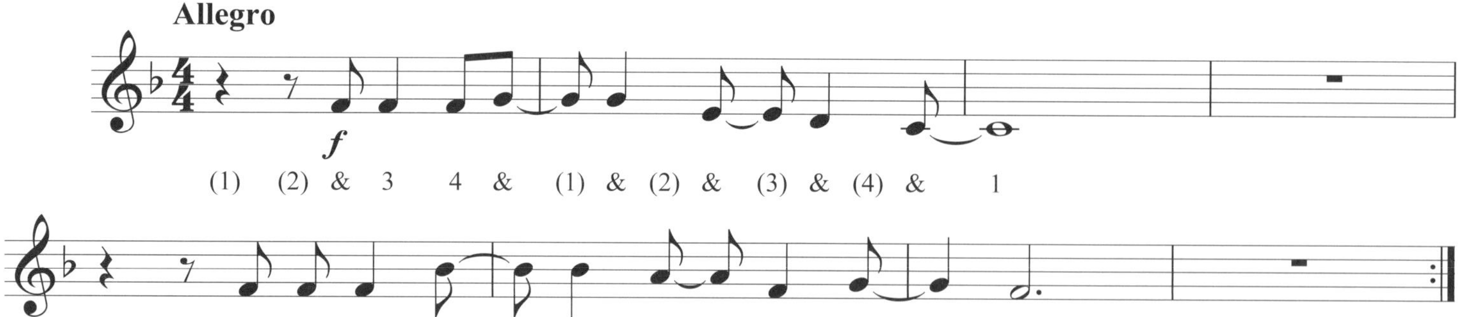

NOWHERE MAN

Words and Music by John Lennon and Paul McCartney

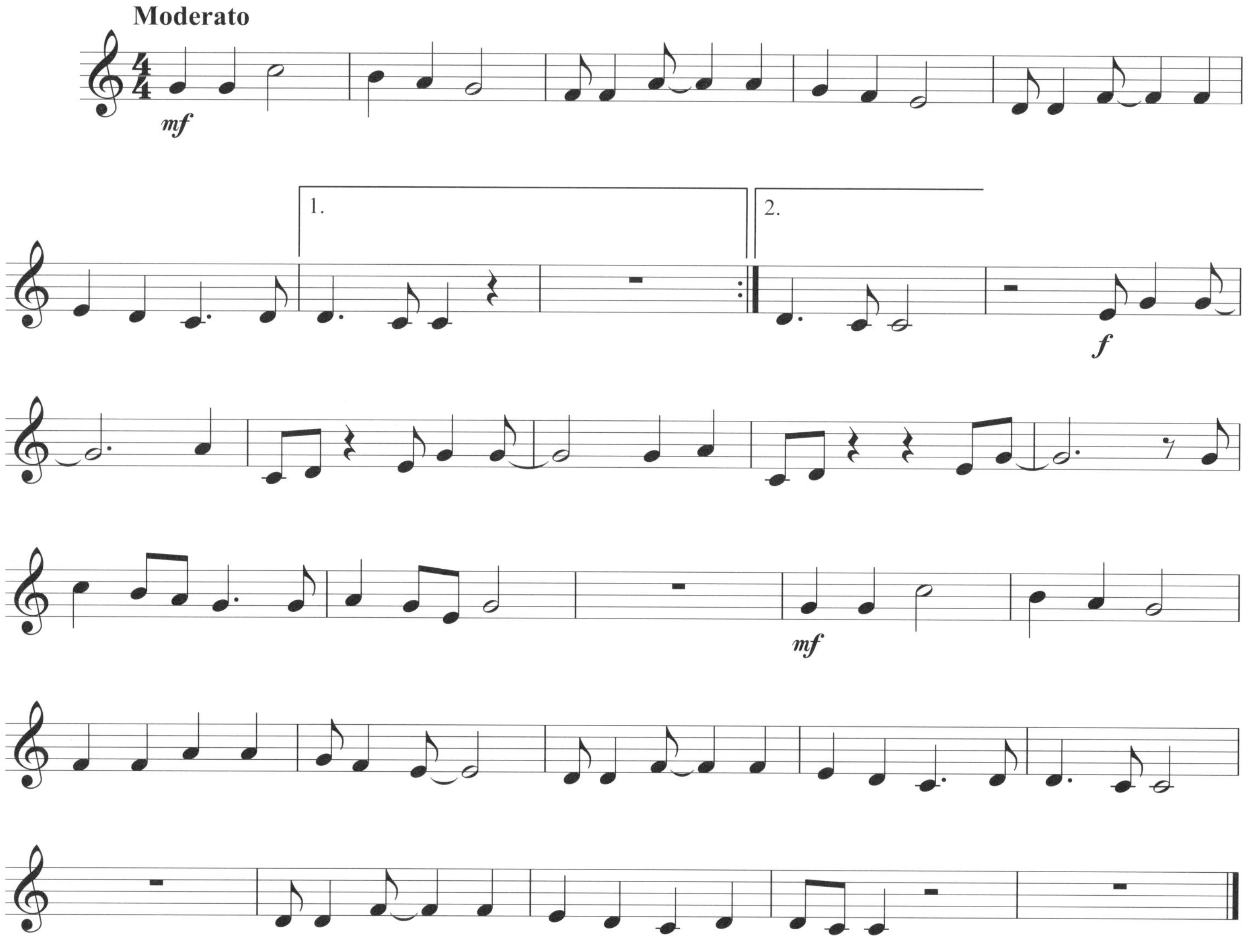

Moderato
mf
1.
2.
f
mf

BLISTER IN THE SUN

Words and Music by Gordon Gano

Allegro

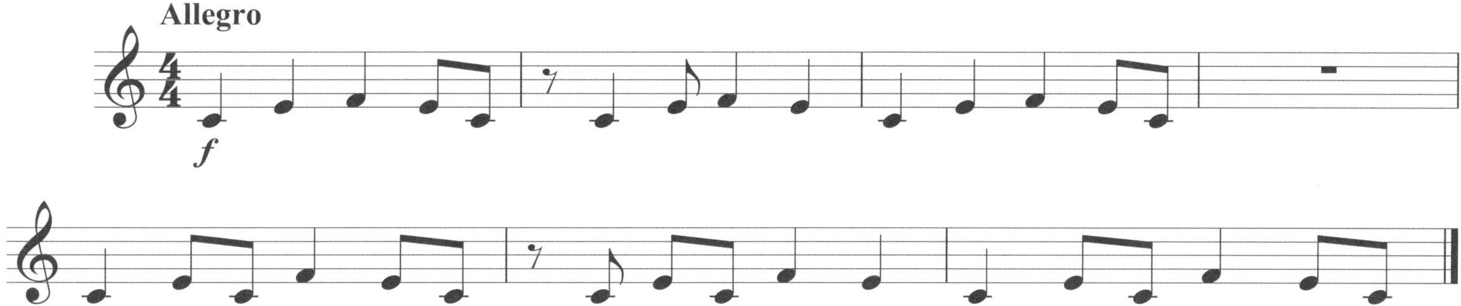

FIREFLIES

Words and Music by Adam Young

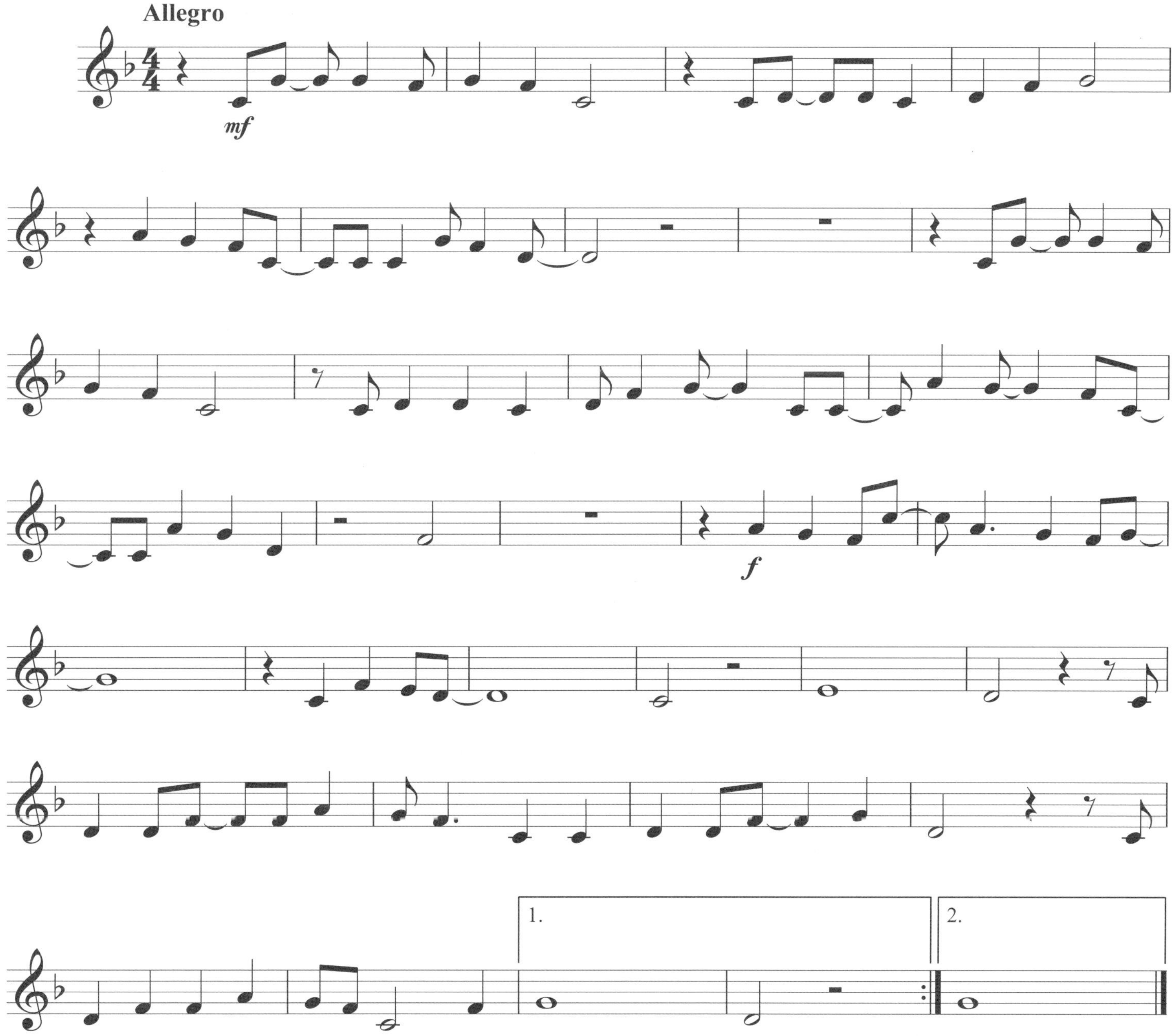
Allegro
1.
2.

TAKE ON ME

Music by Pal Waaktaar and Magne Furuholmne
Words by Pal Waaktaar, Magne Furuholmne and Morton Harket

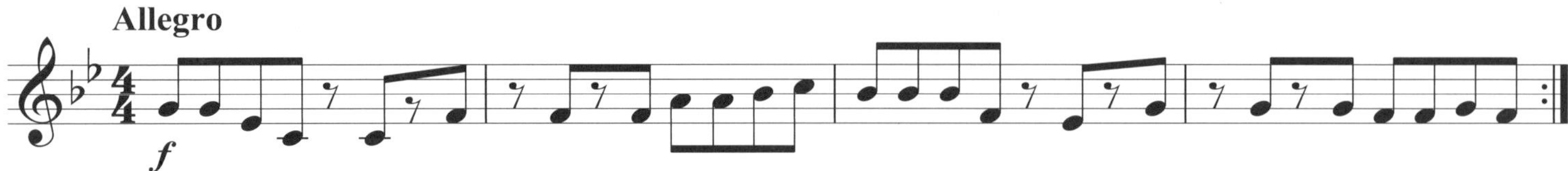

HEY, SOUL SISTER

Words and Music by Pat Monahan, Espen Lind and Amund Bjorklund

Moderato

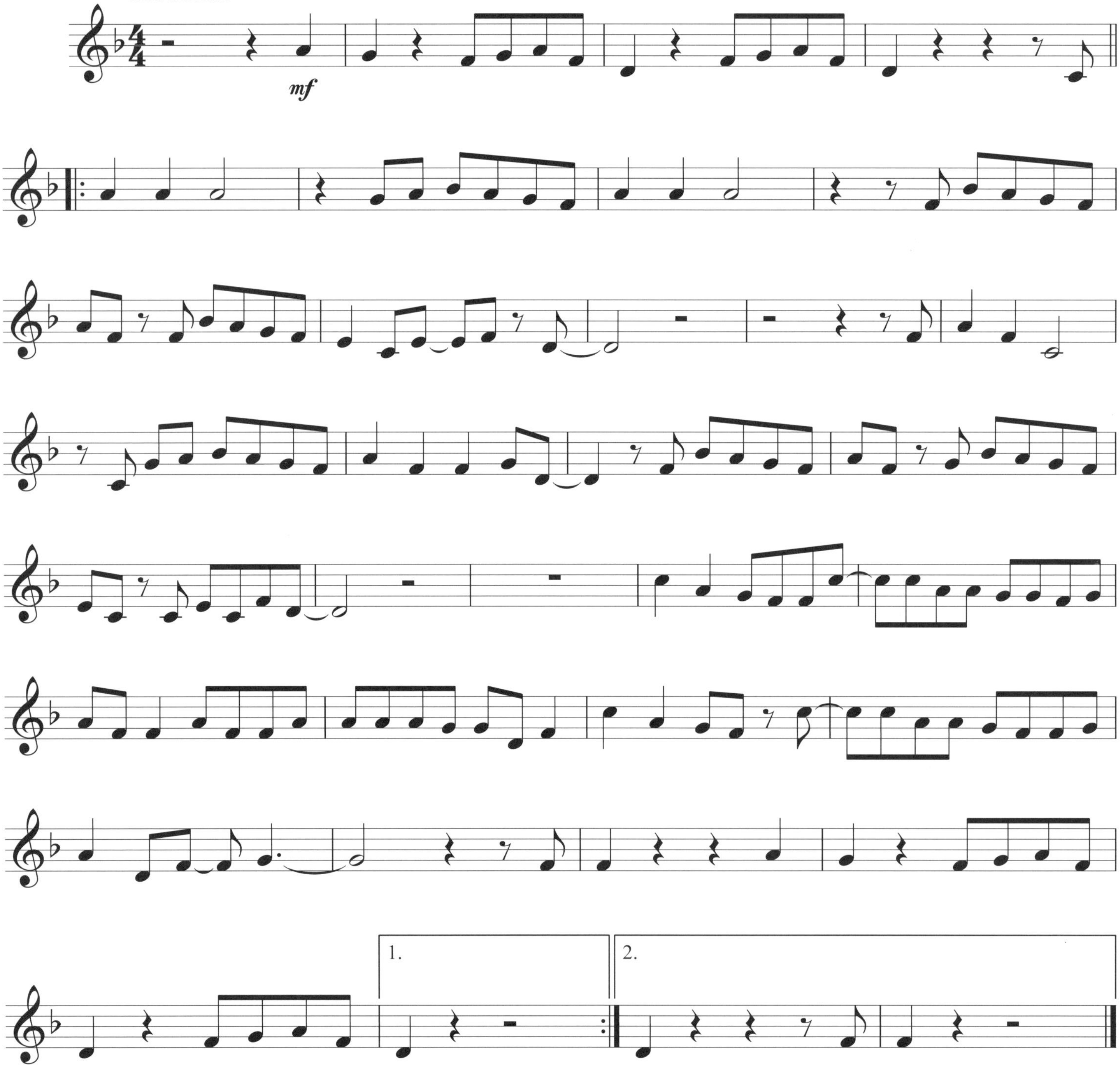

1. 2.

In "Yeah," the first and second half of the next song sound the same because the two eighth notes tied together are the same length as one quarter note.

YEAH!

Words and Music by James Phillips, La Marquis Jefferson, Christopher Bridges, Jonathan Smith and Sean Garrett

Trumpet Talk: Written vs. Sounding PItch

You may be wondering, "Why are most trumpets called 'B-flat' trumpets?" This is because when played, the trumpet sounds one-whole step lower than it is written (or two adjacent piano keys). In other words, if you play a C on the trumpet, a B♭ on a piano will sound. This can get confusing if you have a tuner or app on your phone and you are trying to tune your instrument; the pitch that is displayed will always be one whole step lower than you are playing. Or, if someone is playing music in this book on the piano, it will sound a whole step higher than when you play it on your trumpet.

For our purposes, we will always work in written pitch. However, sometimes, knowing which note you are playing can be puzzling because there are multiple pitches that can be played with each valve combination. The lingo for trumpet players is to say, "what partial are you in?" Sometimes, you might have to check your pitch on a keyboard or app to get used to how fast to buzz to create a certain pitch.

Let's try an example.

Play a second line G and hold it. We will call this written pitch, or the pitch that you see on the music.

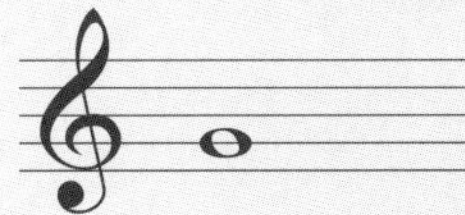

On a tuner or tuner app, a first space F should appear. Sometimes, apps or tuners will show this as F4, or the F above middle C. We call this the sounding pitch.

Perhaps one of the biggest challenges when learning the trumpet is to figure out which "partial" you are playing in. A tuner can help as you get used to knowing how fast to buzz your lips to get the right note out at the right time. A reminder: any note that you identify on a tuner will be one whole-step lower than the written pitch.

Pop Music—AABA Form

Songs from the Broadway and Popular Music worlds are usually comprised of two melodic ideas, labeled A and B. Often, these ideas are eight measures in length. The A theme is repeated twice, followed by the B theme, often referred to as the bridge, as it connects the melodic ideas together. The A theme is restated a third time to complete the melodic material, making the form of the piece of music AABA.

The restatement of the A theme is sometimes altered (A^1), which may result in the form being AA^1BA^1.

DON'T KNOW WHY

Words and Music by Jesse Harris

RIGHT HERE WAITING

Words and Music by Richard Marx

Sometimes, two different dynamics are shown when the music repeats. The dynamics are separated by a hyphen. Play the first dynamic the first time through and play the second dynamic on the repeat.

p-f

CAN CAN

from ORPHEUS IN THE UNDERWORLD

By Jacques Offenbach

HAPPY TOGETHER

Words and Music by Garry Bonner and Alan Gordon

LESSON 9:
Articulations

Staccato

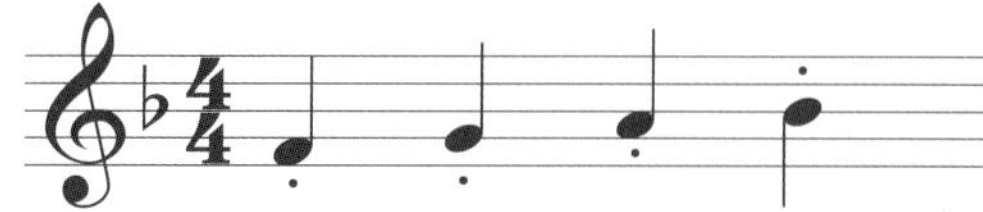

Staccato is an articulation indicating that the notes should be played light and separated.

There should be a brief silence (or separation) between staccato notes.

TOOLBOX

Toolbox Tip: Staccato Tonguing
To play staccato, move your tongue as if you are making the sound "TEEHH."

Staccato tonguing has been described as playing "short" notes, but perhaps a better description would be "light" notes. Many players make the mistake of making a "TUT" sound rather than a "TEEHH" sound with a quick puff of air. It is always better to let the air stop your sound and not your tongue. The goal of a good staccato sound is light and short.

GHOSTBUSTERS

from the Columbia Motion Picture GHOSTBUSTERS
Words and Music by Ray Parker, Jr.

SUNSHINE OF YOUR LOVE

Words and Music by Eric Clapton, Jack Bruce and Pete Brown

KARMA CHAMELEON

Words and Music by George O'Dowd, Jonathan Moss, Michael Craig, Roy Hay and Phil Pickett

THE BANANA BOAT SONG

Jamaican Work Song

TAINTED LOVE

Words and Music by Ed Cobb

Crescendo and Decrescendo

Crescendo: gradually getting louder

Decrescendo: gradually getting softer

A decrescendo may also be called a **diminuendo**. Sometimes these terms are abbreviated ***cresc.***, ***decresc***, and ***dim.***, rather than using their symbols.

New Dynamic

ff

Fortissimo: very loud

THIS IS HALLOWEEN

from THE NIGHTMARE BEFORE CHRISTMAS

Music and Lyrics by Danny Elfman

Allegro

Accent

An **accent** is an articulation indicating to attack the note by playing it stronger.

TOOLBOX

Toolbox Tip: Accent Tonguing

To play an accent, move your tongue as if you are making the sound "TEE." There should be a small amount of space between each note.

OLD TIME ROCK & ROLL

Words and Music by George Jackson and Thomas E. Jones III

LIVIN' ON A PRAYER

Words and Music by Jon Bon Jovi, Desmond Child and Richie Sambora

Moderato

BAD MEDICINE

Words and Music by Jon Bon Jovi, Desmond Child and Richie Sambora

MONY, MONY

Words and Music by Bobby Bloom, Tommy James, Ritchie Cordell and Bo Gentry

Legato

Legato is an articulation indicating to play smooth and connected.

Slur

A **slur** connects two or more notes of any pitch. A slur indicates to play the notes under the slur without tonguing. However, the first note of a slurred section should be tongued.

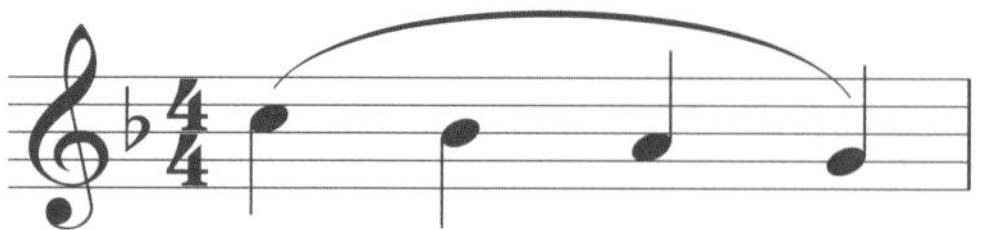

> TOOLBOX
>
> **Toolbox Tip: Slurring**
>
> When you slur notes on the trumpet, the articulation starts normally with the first note, and then the tongue should be out of the way and not interrupt the flow of air until the end of the slur. The valves should be pressed down with authority, just like one would do during normal playing.

LINUS AND LUCY

from A CHARLIE BROWN CHRISTMAS

By Vince Guaraldi

New Note: F♯

DANSE BACCHANALE

from SAMSON ET DALILA (SAMSON AND DELILA)

By Camille Saint-Saens

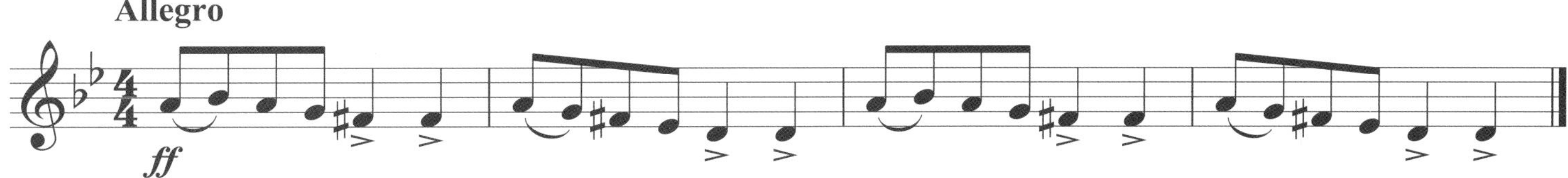

WHEN THE SAINTS GO MARCHING IN

Words by Katherine E. Purvis • Music by James M. Black

YESTERDAY

Words and Music by John Lennon and Paul McCartney

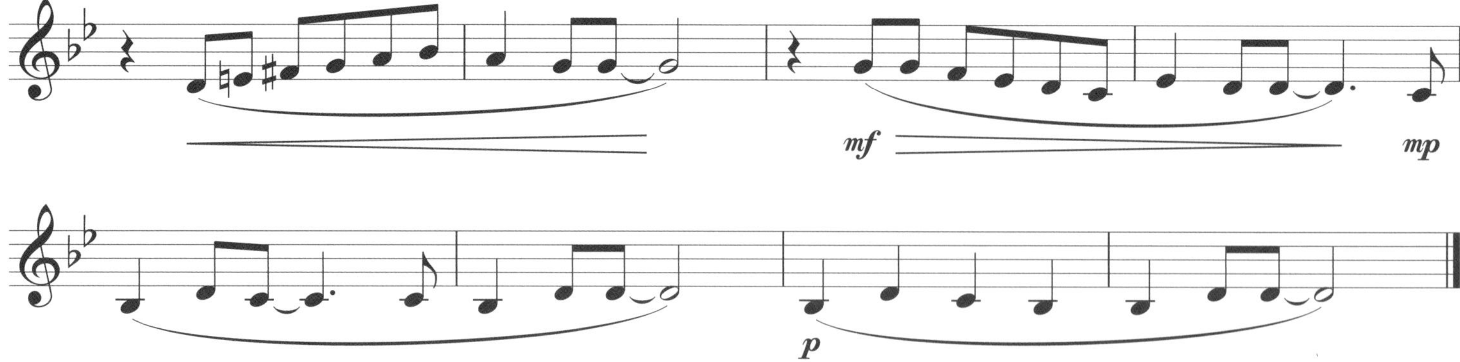

IF I WERE A RICH MAN

from the Musical FIDDLER ON THE ROOF

Words by Sheldon Harnick · Music by Jerry Bock

TOOLBOX

Toolbox Tip: Let's Talk Mutes

Trumpets have the wonderful ability to have a different character of sound by using mutes. All mutes make the sound of the trumpet quieter and may change the tuning slightly. This can be solved by adjusting the tuning slide out a bit.

A **straight mute** is a cone-shaped mute that produces a piercing or nasal-like sound. It is made from aluminum or stone-lined cardboard. It is usually the "go-to" mute for most playing situations where the kind of mute needed is not marked.

A **cup mute** is a larger mute that is almost the same size as the bell of the trumpet. It is also made from aluminum or stone-lined cardboard. It produces a more mellow and smooth sound that is present in much of the modern and jazz repertoire.

A **Harmon mute** (or **wah-wah mute**) is a specialized mute that can be played in two different ways. It is made from aluminum and has a cup-shaped stem that can be used or removed. With the stem out, the Harmon mute is a very tasty mute for jazz. It was often used by the great Miles Davis in many of his recordings. With the stem in, it can produce some great "wah-wah" effects by using the left hand to cover and uncover the cup. The technical term for covering the Harmon mute with your hand is called a "stop" and is notated in the music with a "+" sign above the note. When the hand is removed, the mute is played open and is notated with a "o" sign above the note.

A **plunger** mute is often used in jazz and sometimes in contemporary music. The plunger mute is simply the rubber part of a toilet plunger (unused for its original intent). Like the Harmon mute, the plunger mute is notated with a "stop" and appears in the music with a "+" sign above the note. When the mute is removed, the mute is played open and is notated with a "o" sign above the note.

LESSON 10:
Triplets

Triplets are three notes of equal length that are played the duration of two notes of equal length.

Quarter Note Triplets

3

2 beats   2 beats

Eighth Note Triplets

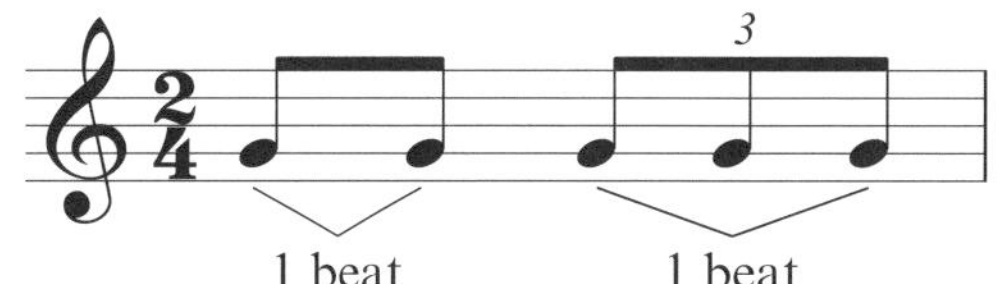

Triplets are often counted like this:

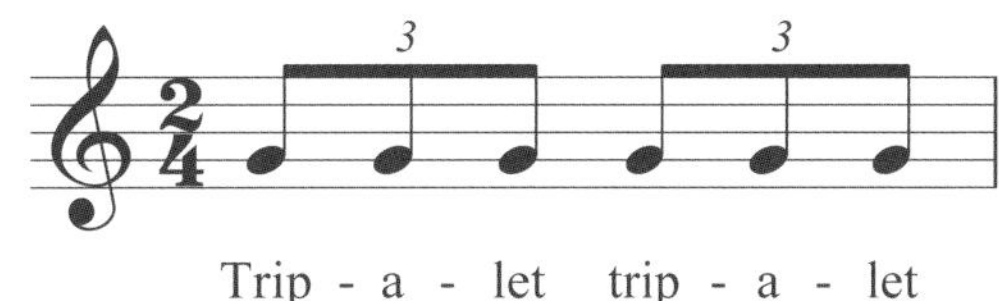

Toolbox Tip: Swing

Swing is a musical style or feeling where eighth notes are not even in length. The first of a group of two eighth notes will feel lightly longer than the second note. The feeling is best described as a triplet, where the first eighth note receives two of the triplet's parts, and the second eighth note receives the final part of the triplet. The final part of the triplet is sometimes referred to as the "back beat." These notes are usually played very smoothly, and the style is best imitated by saying "doo-bah, doo-bah, doo-bah."

Swing sounds like...

...but looks like

TOOLBOX

SEVEN NATION ARMY

Words and Music by Jack White

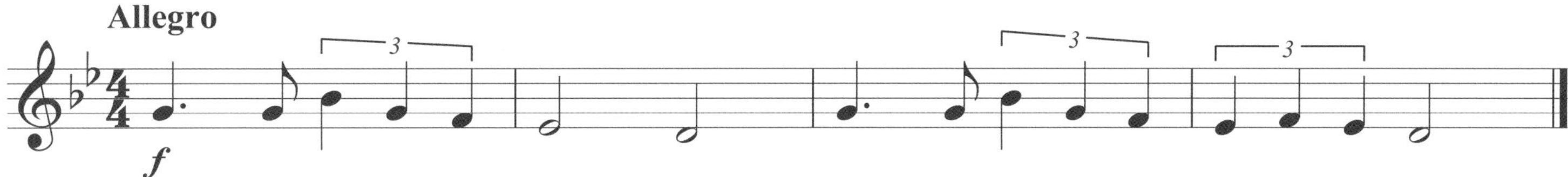

SUMMERTIME

from PORGY AND BESS®

Music and Lyrics by George Gershwin, DuBose and Dorothy Heyward and Ira Gershwin

Optional – this can be played with a Harmon mute without stem.

Tenuto

Tenuto is an articulation that indicates that the note should be held for its full value.

IT DON'T MEAN A THING (IF IT AIN'T GOT THAT SWING)

Words and Music by Duke Ellington and Irving Mills

Optional – this can be played with cup mute throughout.

IRON MAN

Words and Music by Frank Iommi, John Osbourne, William Ward and Terence Butler

SMOKE ON THE WATER

Words and Music by Ritchie Blackmore, Ian Gillan, Roger Glover, Jon Lord and Ian Paice

PUTTIN' ON THE RITZ

Words and Music by Irving Berlin

I CAN'T TURN YOU LOOSE

Words and Music by Otis Redding

SPONGEBOB SQUAREPANTS THEME SONG

from SPONGEBOB SQUAREPANTS

Words and Music by Mark Harrison, Blaise Smith, Stephen M. Hillenburg and Derek Drymon

CHARIOTS OF FIRE

from the Feature Film CHARIOTS OF FIRE

By Vangelis

Moderato

I'LL BE THERE

Words and Music by Berry Gordy Jr., Hal Davis, Willie Hutch and Bob West

Pianissimo

pp

Pianissimo is an indication to play very quietly.

Ritardando

Ritardando: gradually slow down. Often abbreviated as "rit."

Fermata

Fermata: hold for a longer, unspecified amount of time.

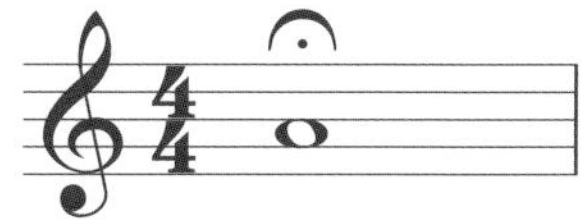

When playing a note with a **fermata**, hold the note longer than usual than its usual duration. Fermatas can also be placed over rests.

IN THE HALL OF THE MOUNTAIN KING

from PEER GYNT

By Edvard Grieg

MORNING HAS BROKEN

Words by Eleanor Farjeon • Music by Cat Stevens

THE WANDERER

Words and Music by Ernest Maresca

THE WAY YOU LOOK TONIGHT

from SWING TIME

Words by Dorothy Fields • Music by Jerome Kern

SWEET CAROLINE

Words and Music by Neil Diamond

LESSON 11:
Lip Slurs

Most brass players like to do **lip slurs**, especially when warming up, to increase flexibility in their lips and to begin to be able to identify pitches. Lip slurs is when you slur between multiple notes that use the same fingering. The notes change by adjusting your embouchure.

Notes that have the same valve combination but have different pitches are part of the **harmonic series.** To get higher notes to sound, your air speed must increase as your aperture gets smaller. This pressurizes your air and allows the higher notes to come out. The individual notes in one particular valve combination are called **partials.** The example below shows what notes are available if a trumpet player plays only open (no valves down).

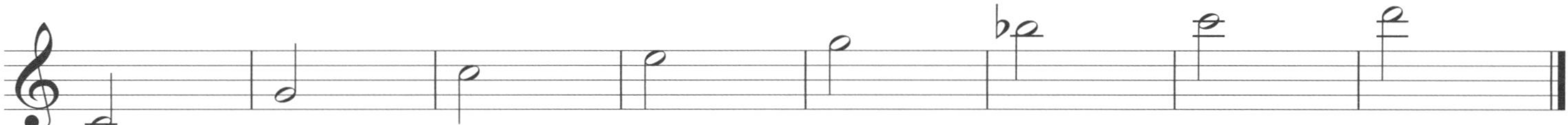

Notice that as you go up in pitch, the interval (space) between the notes gets smaller and smaller. Theoretically, there are an unlimited number of pitches in each harmonic series. The best trumpet players can play all these notes, and higher! Your ability to play higher notes will become much easier if you take the time to do these exercises as a warmup before your practice session. It is helpful if you can do each lip slur exercise with each valve combination.

Play these written pitches below and try to move between them by changing how fast your lips buzz. Try to do the exercise all in one breath, and also try not to stop playing between the notes. Do this first exercise as slowly as you can without running out of breath. Please note that as you progress through these exercises, some of the lower notes have not been revealed yet. You can still play them though as you descend and add valves.

Next, we can incorporate all the valve combinations into a warm-up exercise that is popular with many players. We will descend by one-half step (or by one key on the keyboard) and keep that valve down through the hole line. We often describe this exercise as descending chromatically. The tempo should be fairly slow.

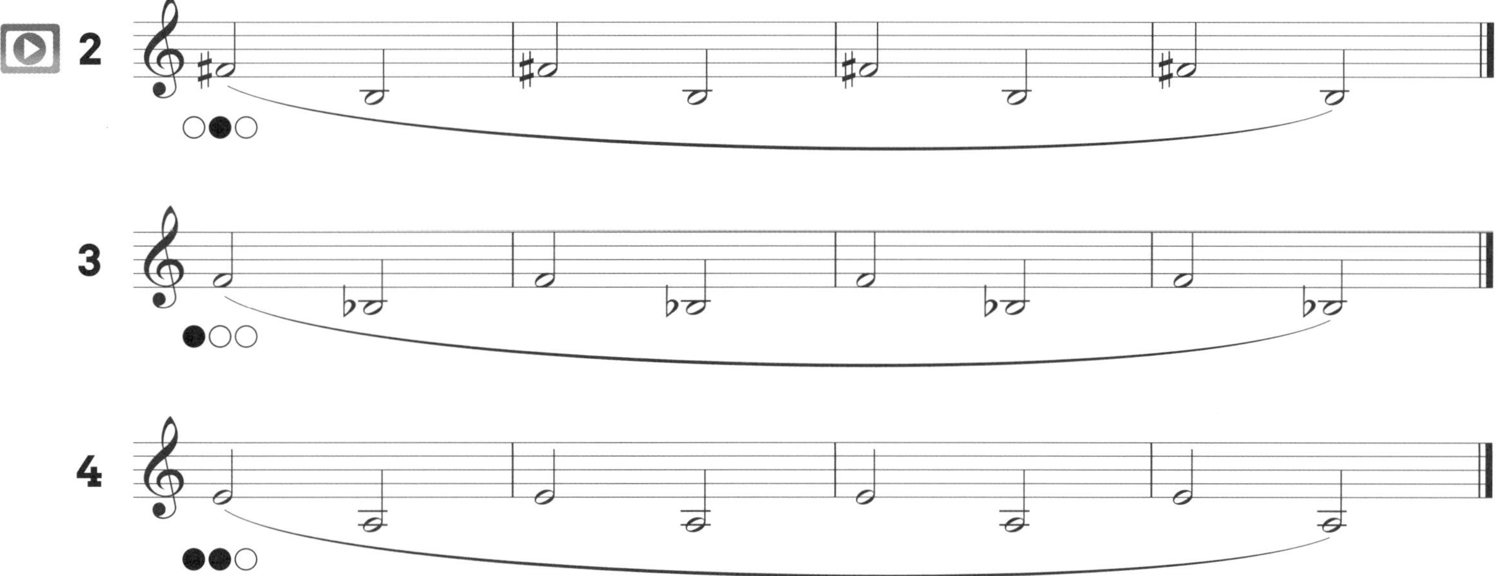

The next group of slurs follows the same pattern but begins one ***partial*** higher.

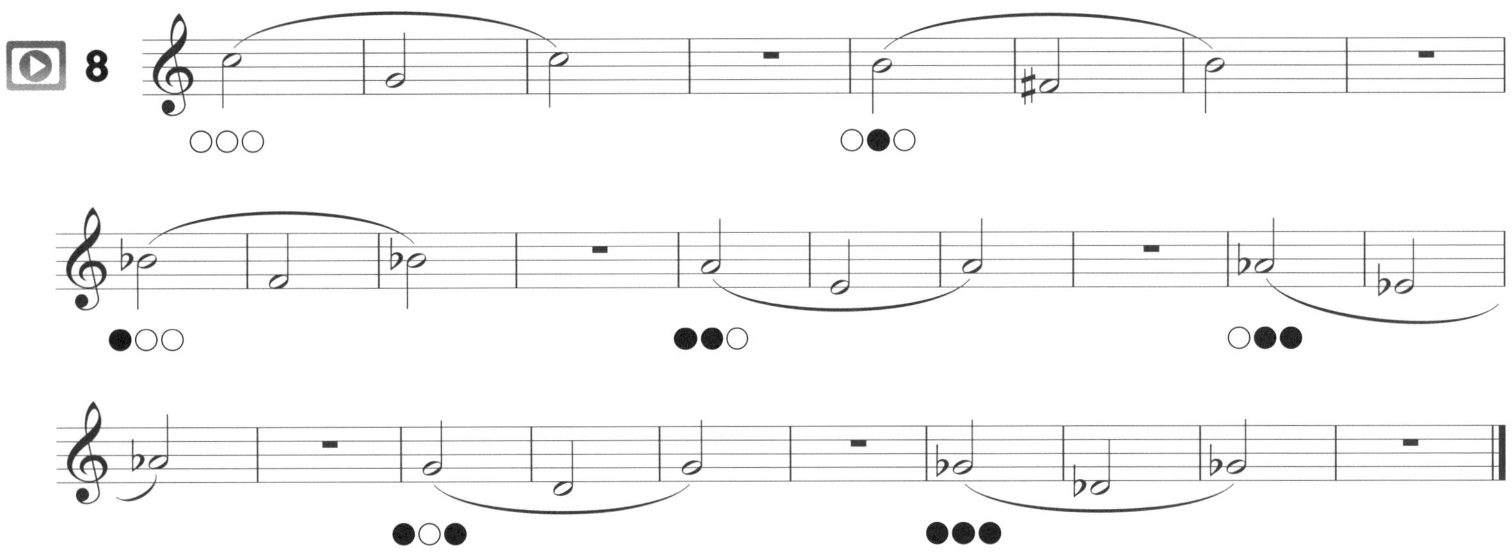

Remember: these (and all lip slurs) can be played at any speed. Begin with long tones, focusing on making the notes change only by changing your air speed, NOT by using your tongue. Once you have control over the lip slurs, you can begin to play them faster for greater technical control and increased fluency. The smoother you can make the slur, the more your technique will improve.

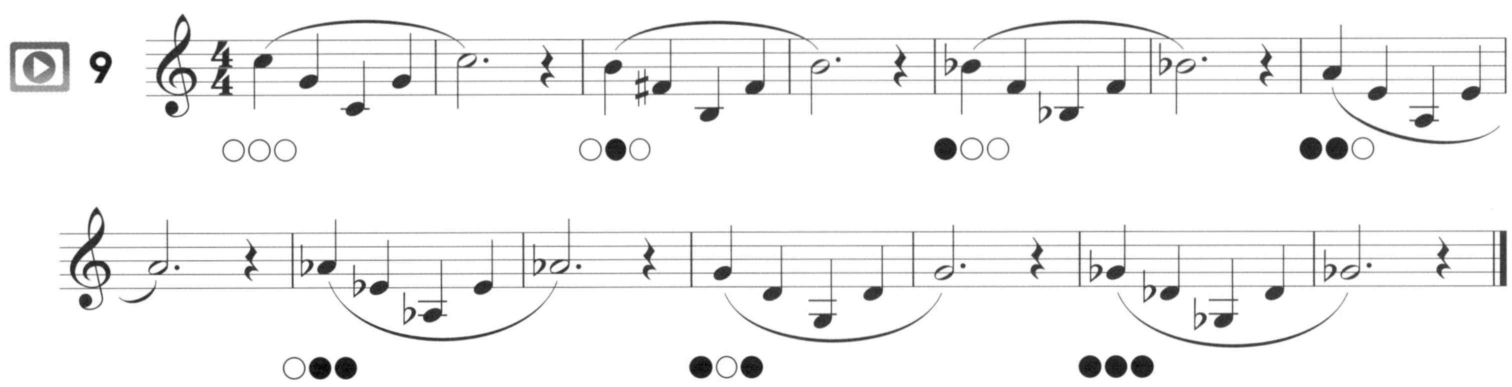

10
11
12

LESSON 12:
Vibrato

Vibrato is a technique used by trumpet players to bend the pitch up and down and to warm up the quality—often called the timbre (TAM-ber)—of the sound. Vibrato is used in solo passages and in solo repertoire, but not so much in ensemble playing. Normally, vibrato is used on longer or more sustained notes. The use of vibrato is a personal choice and is variable depending on the player's taste and the type or genre of the music being played. Most everyone can recall a trumpet solo with vibrato. The type of vibrato used in a Mariachi band might be very different than the vibrato of an orchestral player.

There are two types of vibrato that trumpet players use: hand vibrato and jaw vibrato. Jaw vibrato is most commonly used and can be accomplished by moving your jaw slightly as if you are chewing gum, or saying "wah, wah, wah, wah..."

Vibrato Exercises: Pulses in the Sound

Play the whole note written, pulsing/bending the pitch at the speed of the stemmed notes. Do not tongue the stemmed notes—this is the speed the notes should bend.

Repeat the exercise on several pitches of your choice.

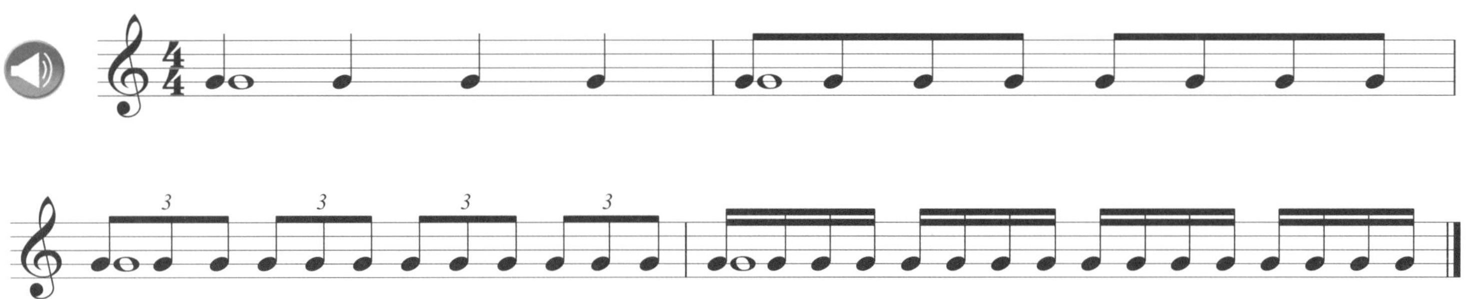

Practice vibrato during the longer notes on this familiar piece.

LULLABY

By Johannes Brahms

UNFORGETTABLE

Words and Music by Irving Gordon

THE LION SLEEPS TONIGHT

New Lyrics and Revised Music by George David Weiss, Luigi Creatore and Hugo Peretti

LESSON 13:
Compound Rhythm

New Time Signature: 6/8

6 = 6 beats in each measure
8 = eighth note receives one beat

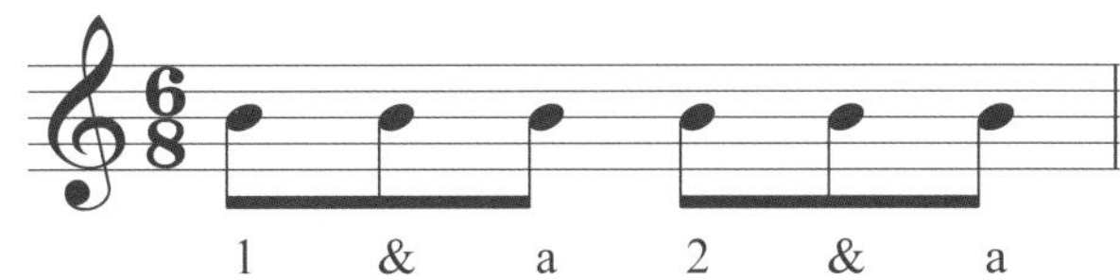

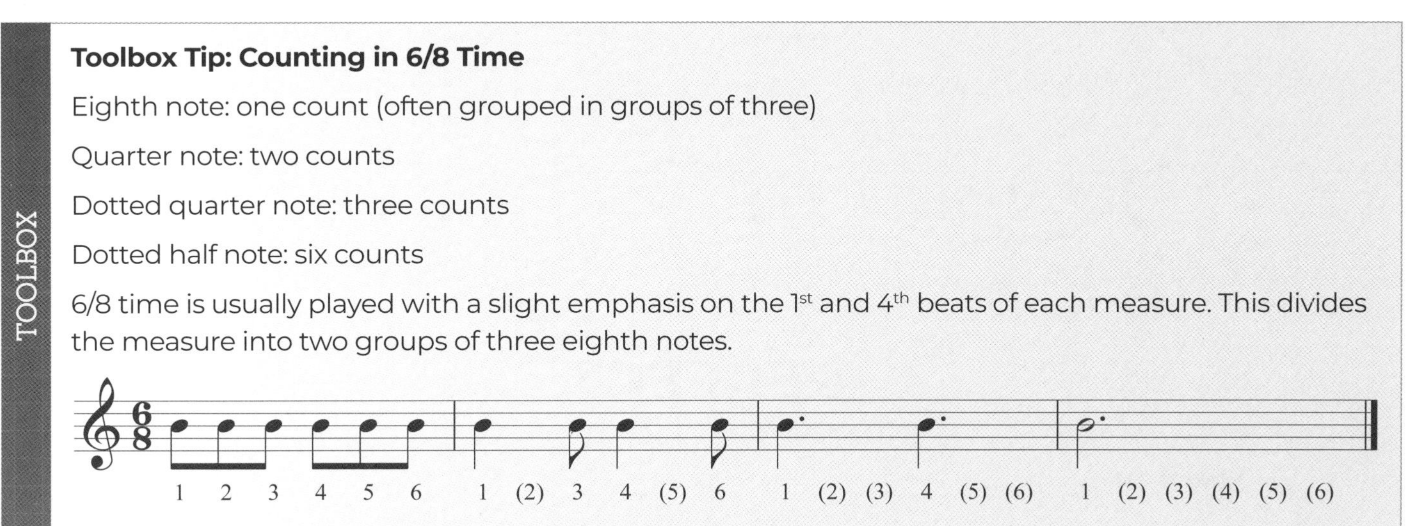

TOOLBOX

Toolbox Tip: Counting in 6/8 Time

Eighth note: one count (often grouped in groups of three)

Quarter note: two counts

Dotted quarter note: three counts

Dotted half note: six counts

6/8 time is usually played with a slight emphasis on the 1st and 4th beats of each measure. This divides the measure into two groups of three eighth notes.

Tempos

Often, in popular music, tempos are written in contemporary terms, rather than in Italian as had been done with earlier styles of music. Rather than writing "Allegro," they might write "Driving Rock," or "Fast." Moderato could be notated as "Freely." Adagio could be "Slowly."

YOU AND ME

Words and Music by Jude Cole and Jason Wade

Slowly (In 6)
mp
mf

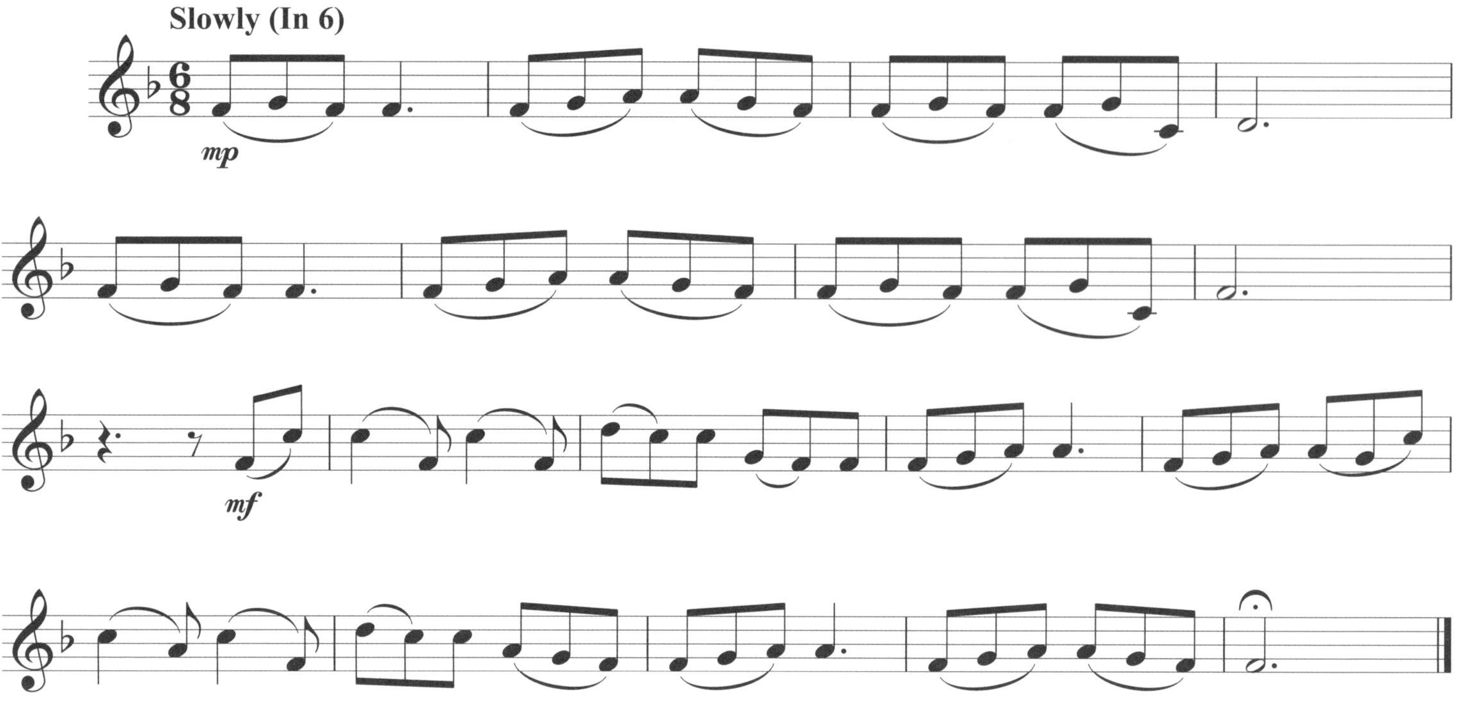

PERFECT

Words and Music by Ed Sheeran

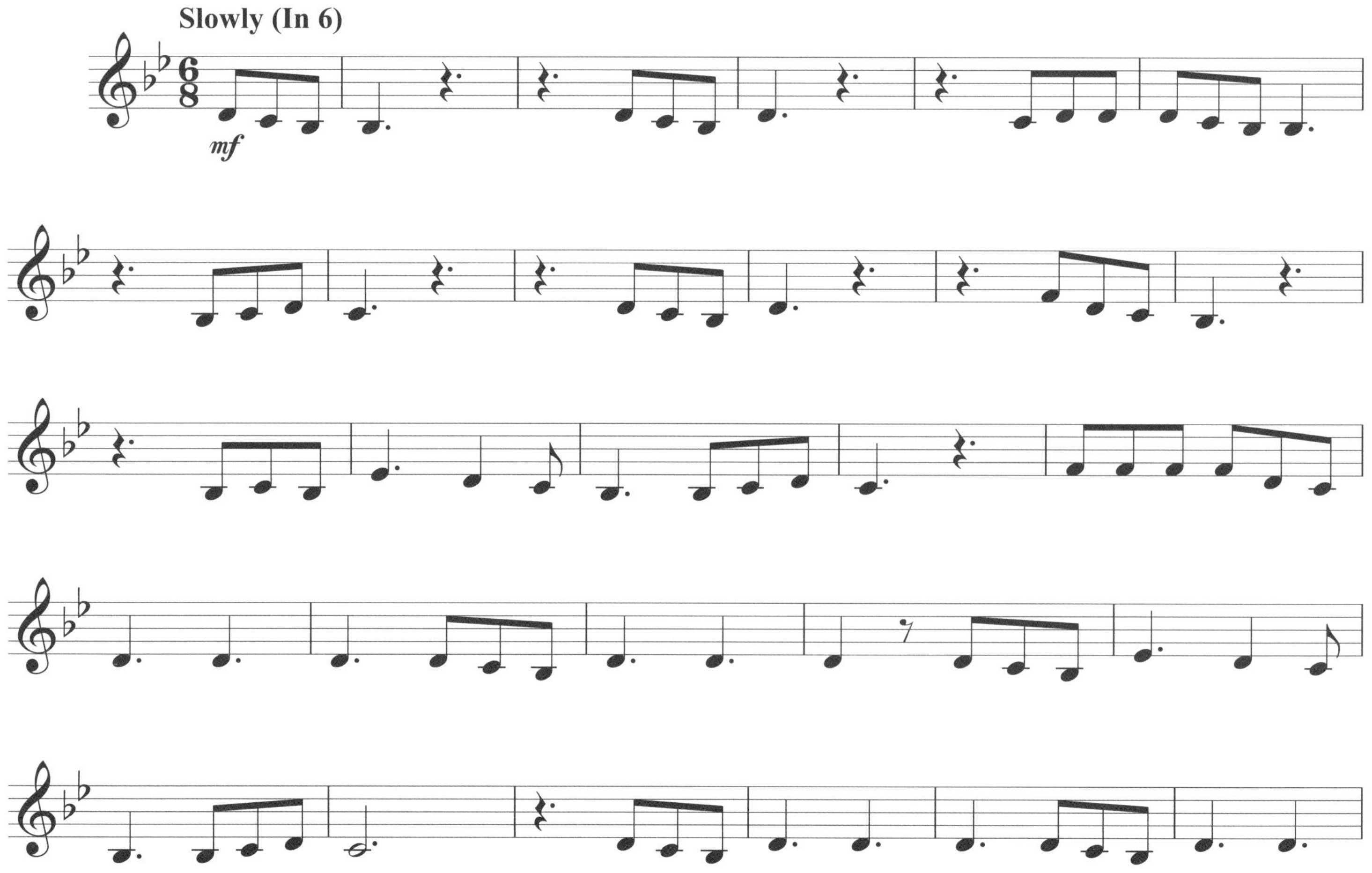
Slowly (In 6)
mf

TOOLBOX

Toolbox Tip: 6/8 Time Felt in Two

In faster music, the two primary beats will make the music feel like it is counted in two, with a dotted quarter note receiving one beat.

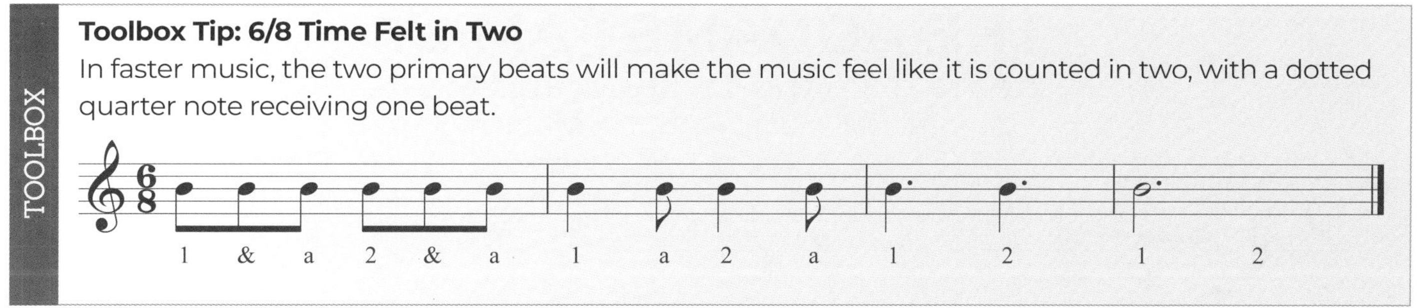

ROW, ROW, ROW YOUR BOAT

Traditional

ITSY BITSY SPIDER

Traditional

Moderato
mf

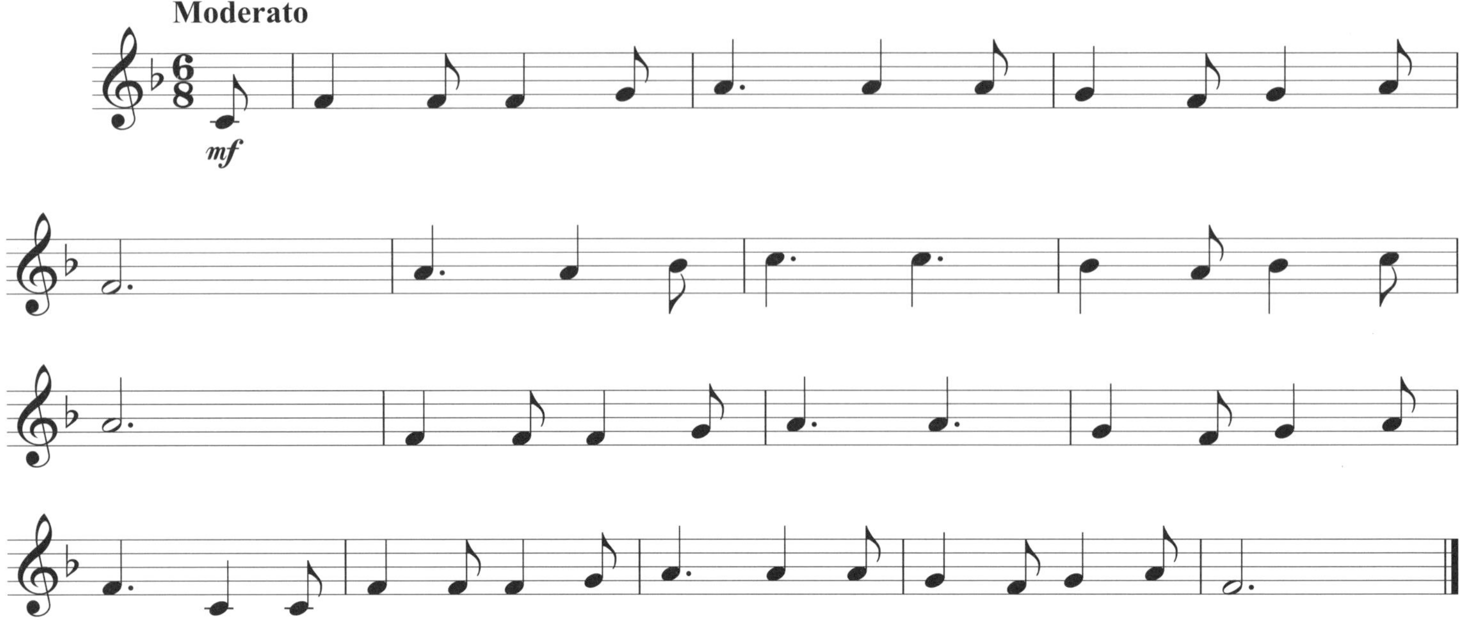

THE ADDAMS FAMILY

Theme from the TV Show and Movie

Music and Lyrics by Vic Mizzy

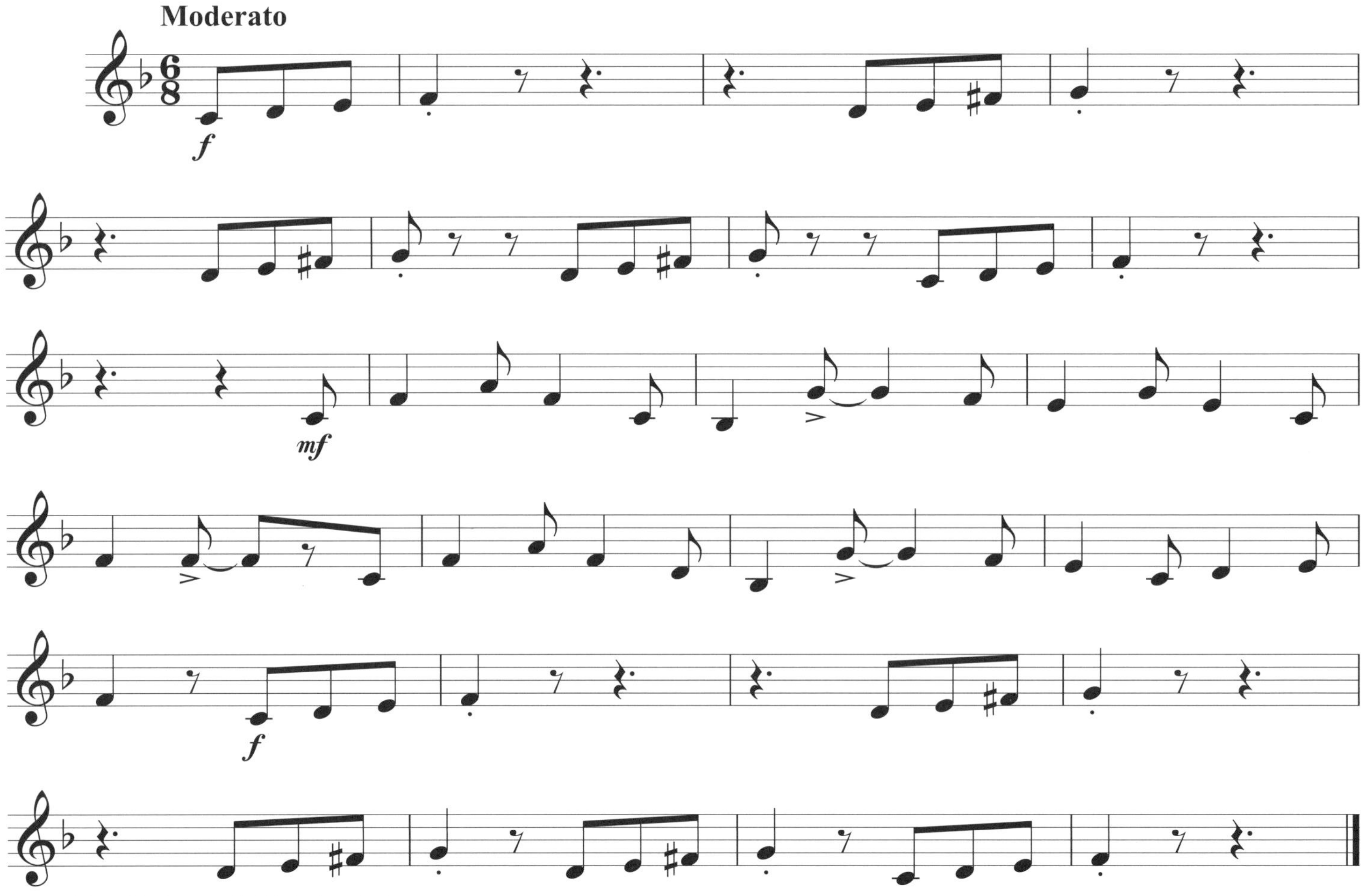
Moderato
f
mf
f

D.C. Al Fine

When you reach the **D.C. al Fine**, return back to the beginning of the piece and stop playing when you reach the Fine (pronounced "FEE-nay"). You do not stop at the Fine the first time.

OYE COMO VA

Words and Music by Tito Puente

WE'RE NOT GONNA TAKE IT

Words and Music by Daniel Dee Snider

UNCHAINED MELODY

from the Motion Picture UNCHAINED

Lyric by Hy Zaret • Music by Alex North

LESSON 14:
More Advanced Rhythms

Sixteenth Note

A **sixteenth note** receives 1/4 of a beat of sound. Often, they are paired in groups of two or four notes.

THE GOOD, THE BAD, AND THE UGLY (MAIN TITLE)

By Ennio Morricone

Sixteenth Note Variations

Many songs incorporate sixteenth notes but use variations of sixteenth notes and eighth notes or rests. Some of the more common include:

UNDER PRESSURE

Words and Music by Freddie Mercury, John Deacon, Brian May, Roger Taylor and David Bowie

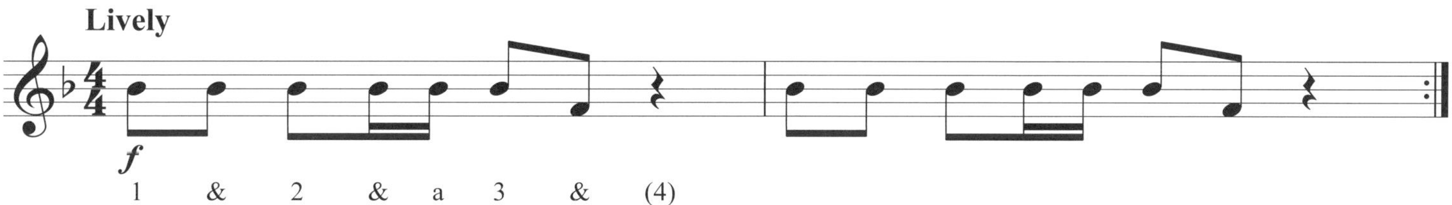

Sixteenth Note Rest

𝄿

A **sixteenth rest** takes up the same rhythmic time as a sixteenth note (1/4 of a beat).

WALK THIS WAY

Words and Music by Steven Tyler and Joe Perry

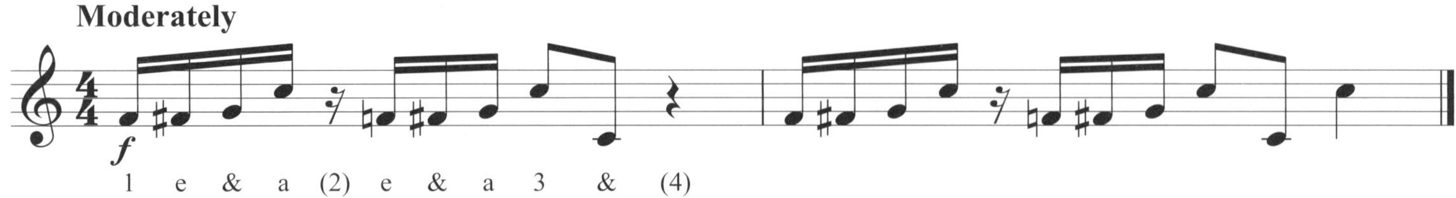

ALL BLUES

By Miles Davis

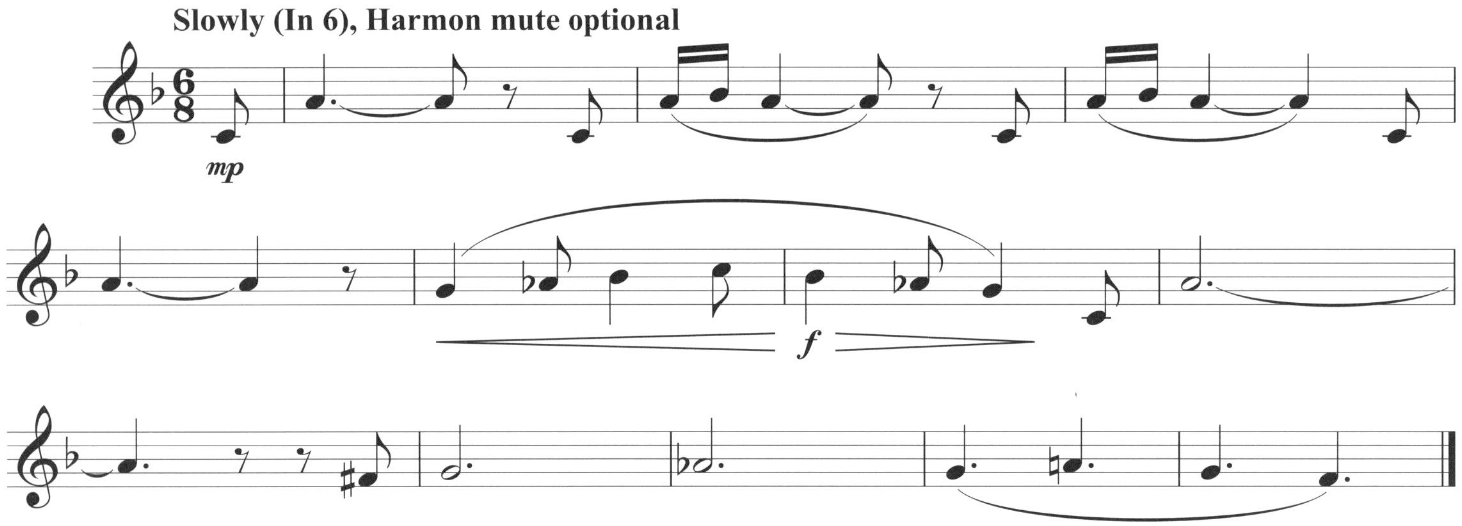

LULLABY

By Johannes Brahms

1.
2.

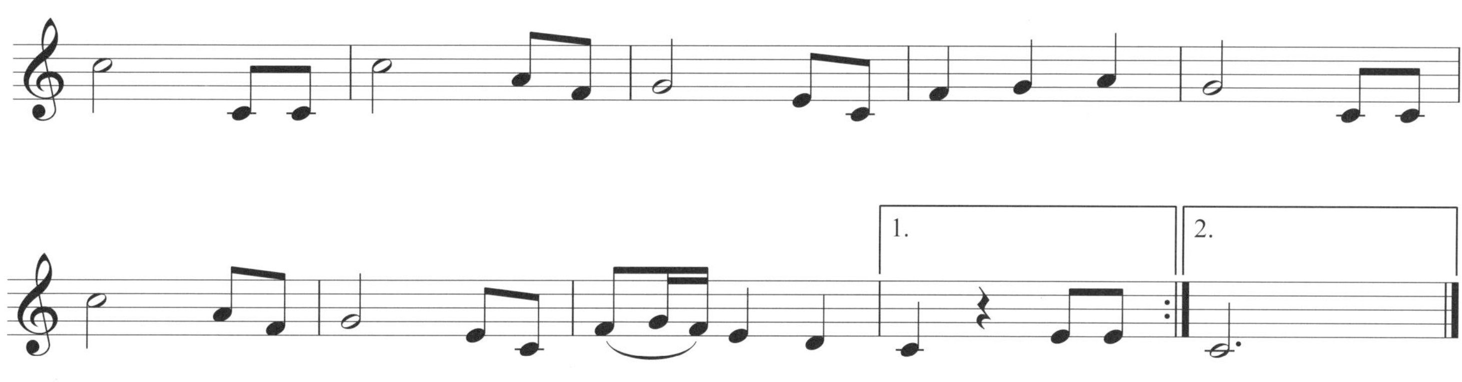

ALL STAR

Words and Music by Greg Camp

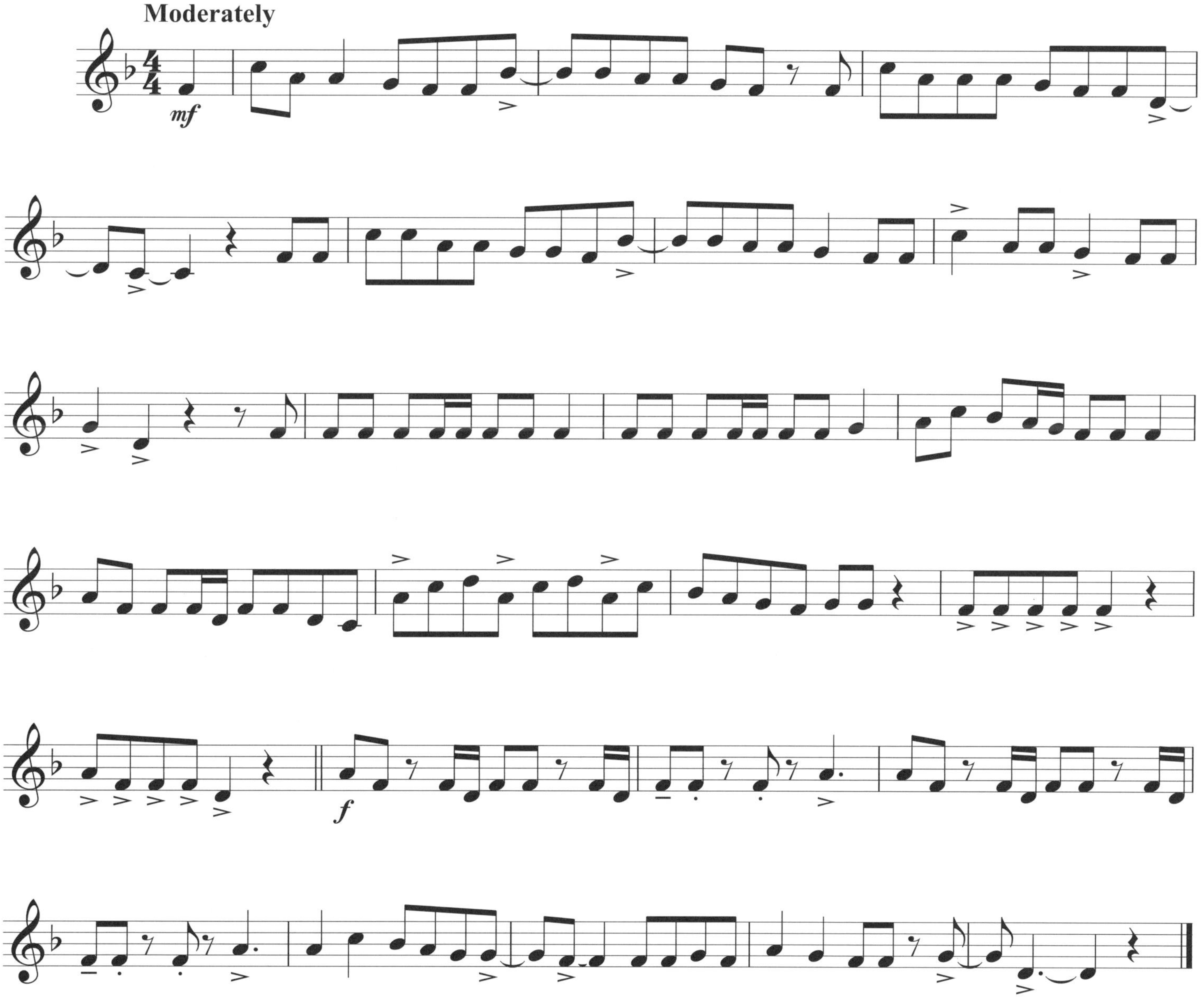
Moderately
mf
f

Dotted Eighth/Sixteenth

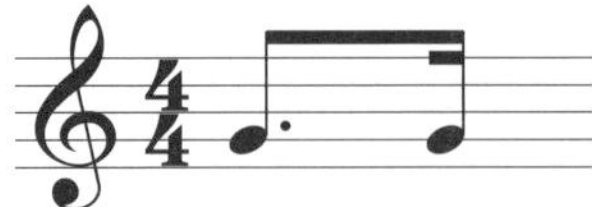

Recall from earlier, the dot adds half the value of the existing note. A **dotted eighth note** is worth 3/4 of a beat.

EYE OF THE TIGER

Theme from ROCKY III

Words and Music by Frank Sullivan and Jim Peterik

Maestoso: majestically

Largo: very slow

WEDDING MARCH

from A MIDSUMMER NIGHT'S DREAM

By Felix Mendelssohn

FUNERAL MARCH

from PIANO SONATA IN B-FLAT MINOR, OP. 35

By Fryderyk Chopin

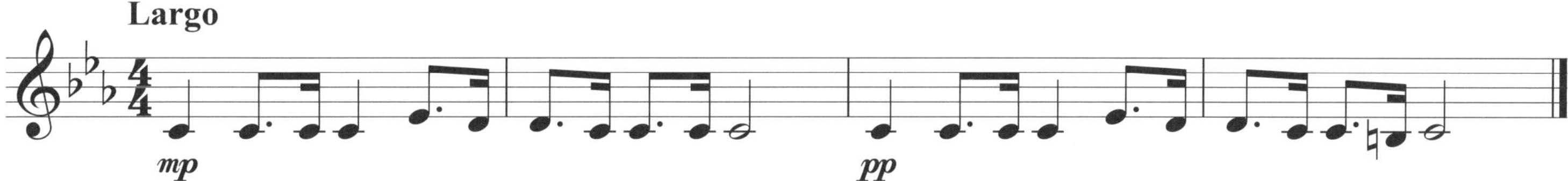

Multiple Measure Rest

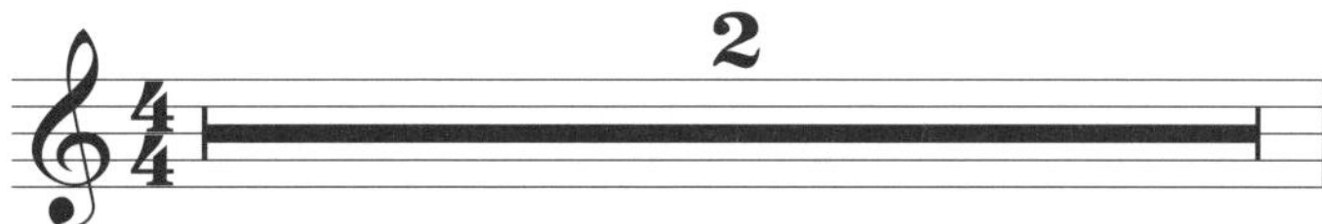

When the music indicates music beyond one measure in length, they may be written as a single measure with a number noted above. That number indicates the quantity of measures to rest.

I WISH

Words and Music by Stevie Wonder

A tempo: return to the previous tempo

Rallentando: gradually slow down (similar to ritardando)

Molto ritardando: gradually slow down very much

THAT'S AMORÉ (THAT'S LOVE)

from the Paramount Picture THE CADDY

Words by Jack Brooks · Music by Harry Warren

DANNY BOY

Words by Frederick Edward Weatherly · Traditional Irish Folk Melody

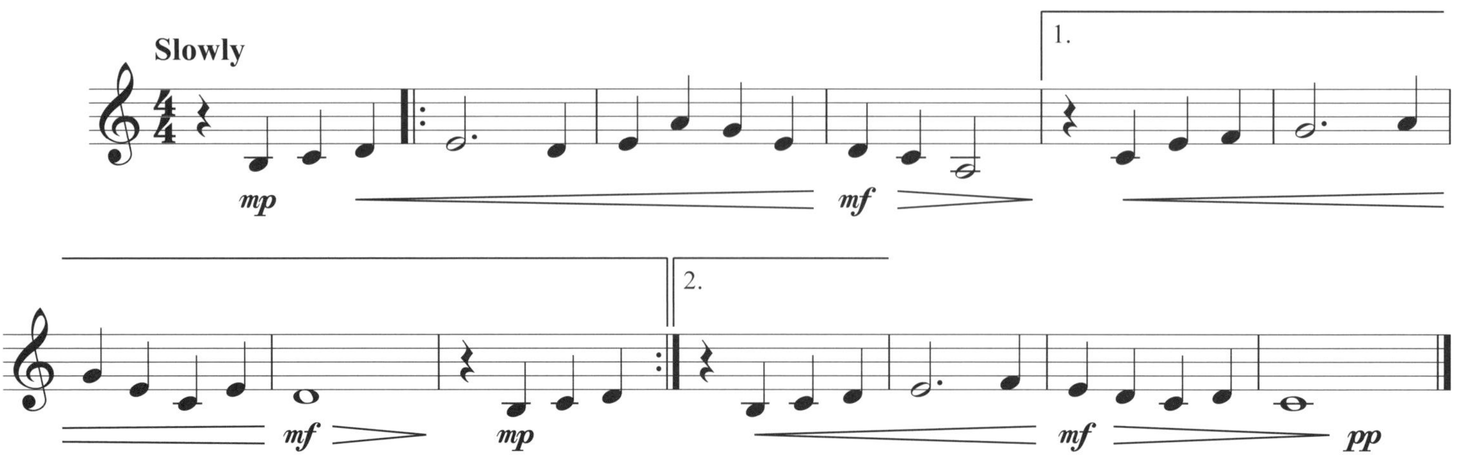

I STILL HAVEN'T FOUND WHAT I'M LOOKING FOR

Words and Music by U2

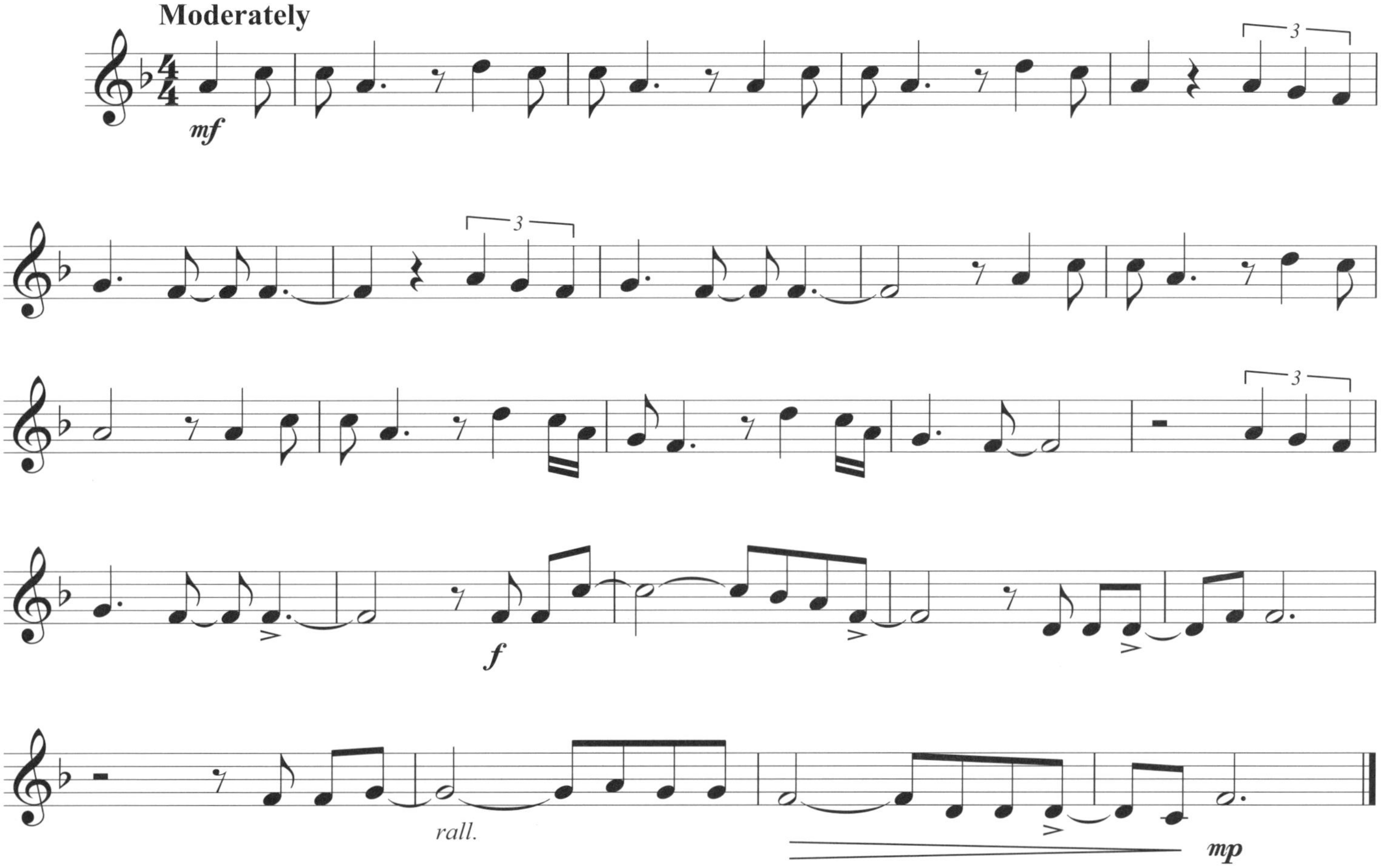
Moderately
mf
3
f
rall.
mp

OVER THE RAINBOW

from THE WIZARD OF OZ

Music by Harold Arlen • Lyric by E.Y. "Yip" Harburg

Moderato
mf
1.
2.
molto rit.

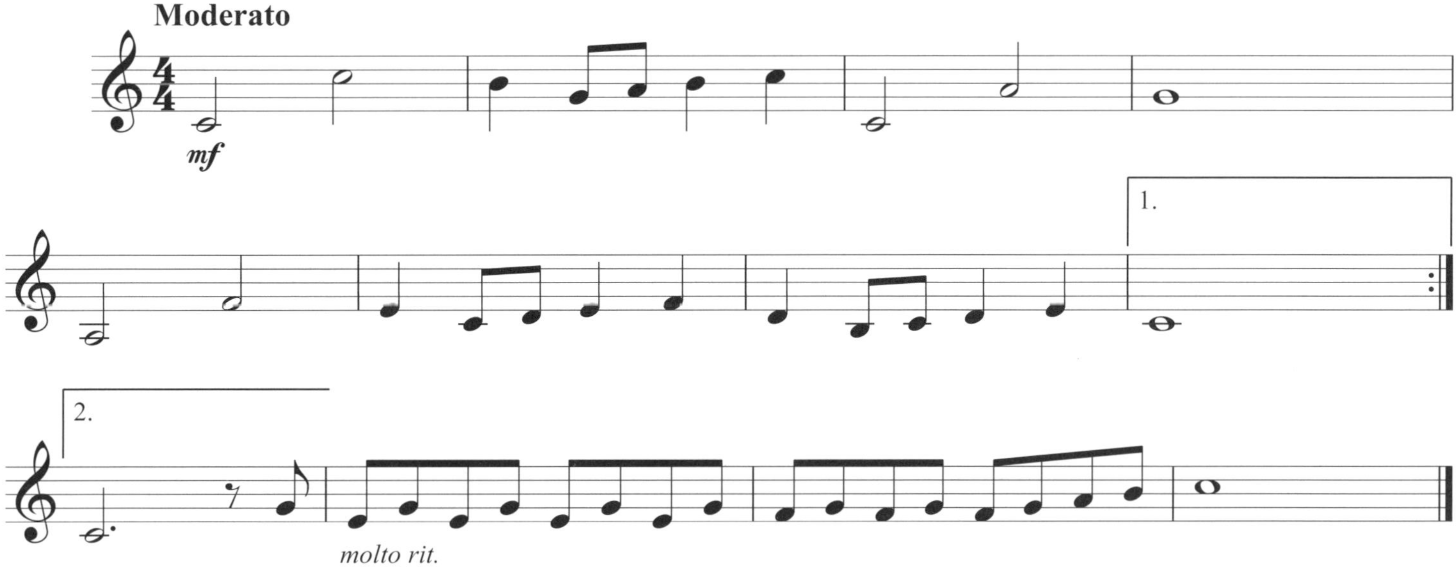

Phrases and Interpretation

A **phrase** is a musical sentence, often two or four measures long.

Follow the direction of the notes to make your phrase more musical. If the notes go higher, add a crescendo. If the notes go lower, add a decrescendo. The goal in music is to add your own subtle changes to dynamics and tempo. This is called **interpretation**.

POLKA DOTS AND MOONBEAMS

Words by Johnny Burke • Music by Jimmy Van Heusen

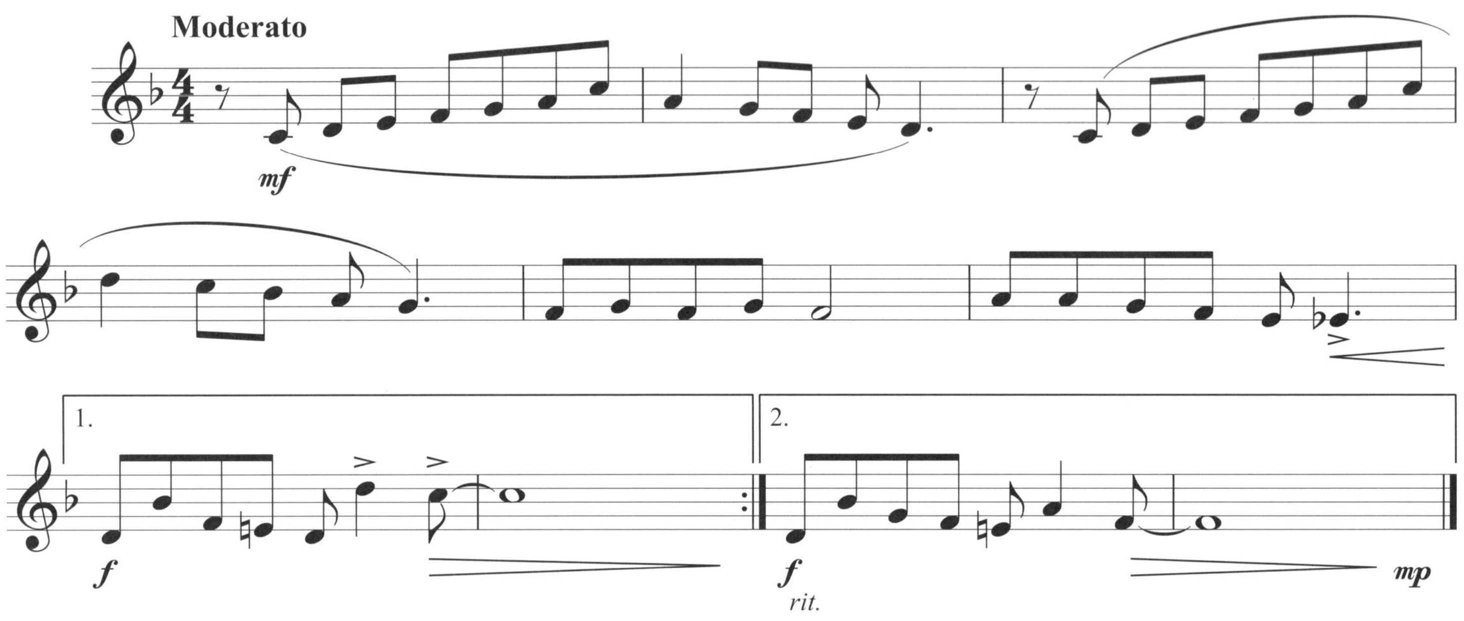

EDELWEISS

from THE SOUND OF MUSIC

Lyrics by Oscar Hammerstein II • Music by Richard Rodgers

p
mp
p
rall.
mf

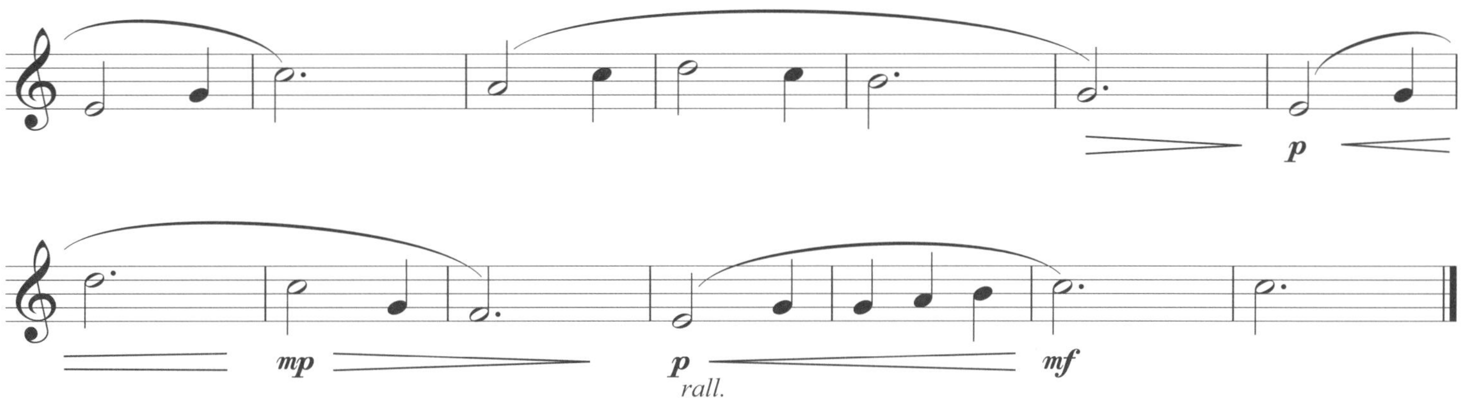

Keep each group of slurs smooth to make a musical **phrase**. Add dynamic contrast and slight tempo changes to make this your own interpretation of the song.

WONDERFUL TONIGHT

Words and Music by Eric Clapton

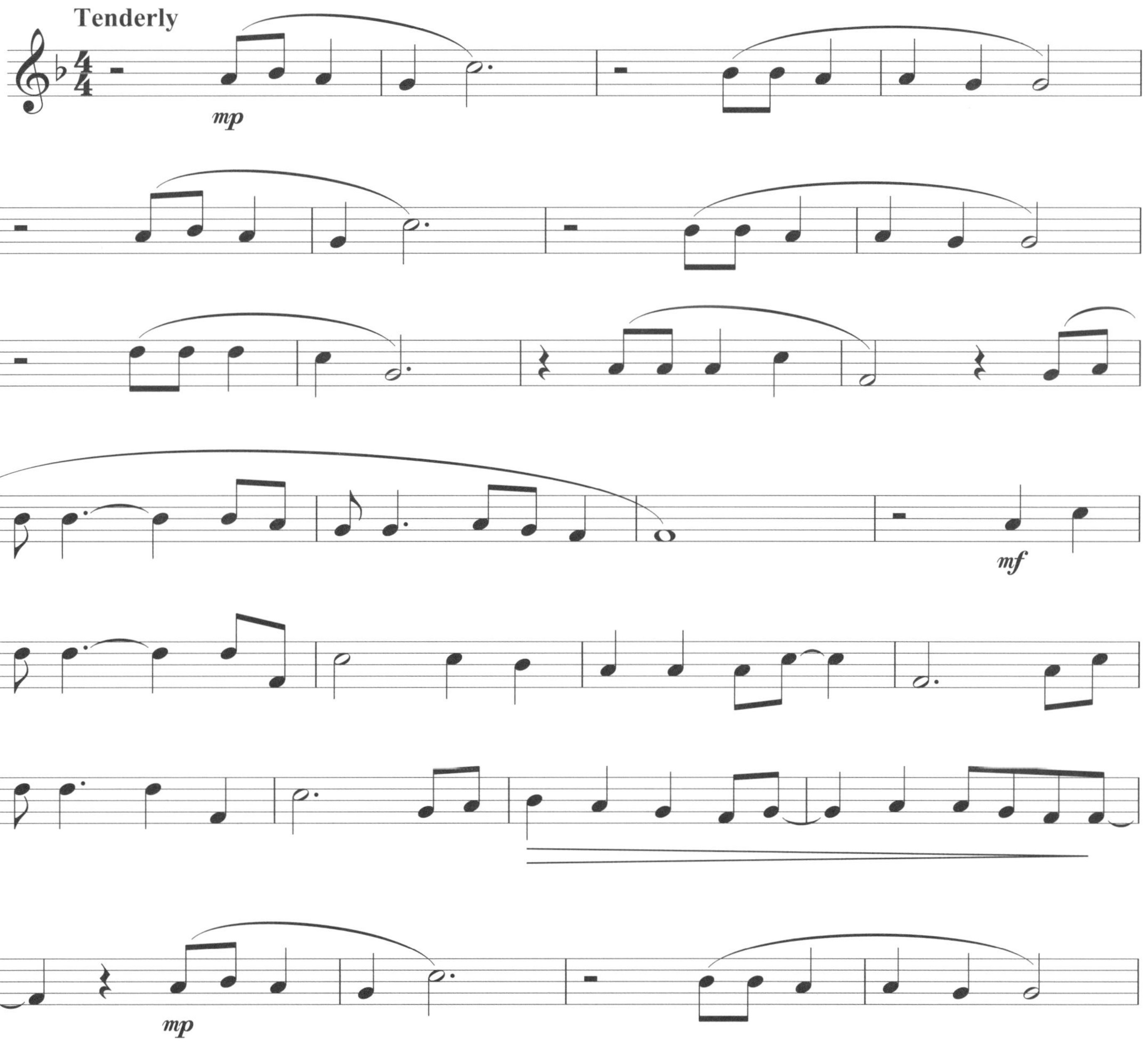
Tenderly
mp
mf
mp

Marcato Accent

A **marcato accent** begins with a strong attack, followed by a decay in sound. There should be a small amount of space (silence) between these notes.

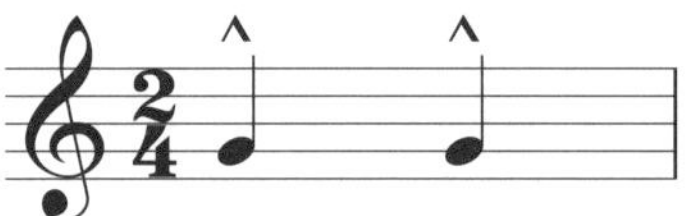

DON'T STOP BELIEVIN'

Words and Music by Steve Perry, Neal Schon and Jonathan Cain

Moderately fast

mf
ff

D.C. al Coda

When you reach the **D.C. al Coda**, return back to the beginning of the piece and play until you reach the "To Coda" marking in the music. Jump down to the Coda (usually near the end of the piece) and play until the end of the song.

⊕ **Coda** = the conclusion

To Coda ⊕

STRANGERS IN THE NIGHT

adapted from A MAN COULD GET KILLED

Words by Charles Singleton and Eddie Snyder · Music by Bert Kaempfert

LESSON 15:
Playing Even Higher

Trumpet Talk: Playing High Notes
Many trumpet players want to expand their range, and this is a lofty goal. As stated earlier in the book, the key is to move air faster and reduce the size of the aperture in the embouchure. Be careful not to make the common mistake of using a lot of tension or forcing the mouthpiece into the lips. Doing this will lead to frustration and a lack of endurance. Daily practice of lip slurs (see lesson 11) is a great way to build range.

New Note: E

New Note: G

MAIN TITLE – APOLLO 13
from APOLLO 13
Composed by James Horner

Enharmonics: A♭ = G♯.

These two pitches sound the same, have the same fingerings, but they are not the same note. One is the **enharmonic** version of the other.

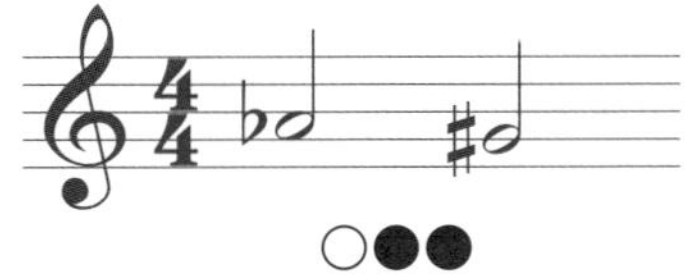

DO-RE-MI

from THE SOUND OF MUSIC

Lyrics by Oscar Hammerstein II • Music by Richard Rodgers

Key Signature: Key of G Major

This key signature has one sharp: F♯

FINAL COUNTDOWN

Words and Music by Joey Tempest

HAIL TO THE CHIEF

By James Sanderson

New Note: F

ONWARD, CHRISTIAN SOLDIERS

Words by Sabine Baring-Gould • Music by Arthur S. Sullivan

Allegro

f

LESSON 16:
Common Time and Cut Time

New Time Signature: Common Time

Common time is another way to notate 4/4 time.

New Note: F♯

CAN'T HELP FALLING IN LOVE

Words and Music by George David Weiss, Hugo Peretti and Luigi Creatore

FANFARE RONDEAU

from SUITE DE SYMPHONIE

By Jean-Joseph Mouret

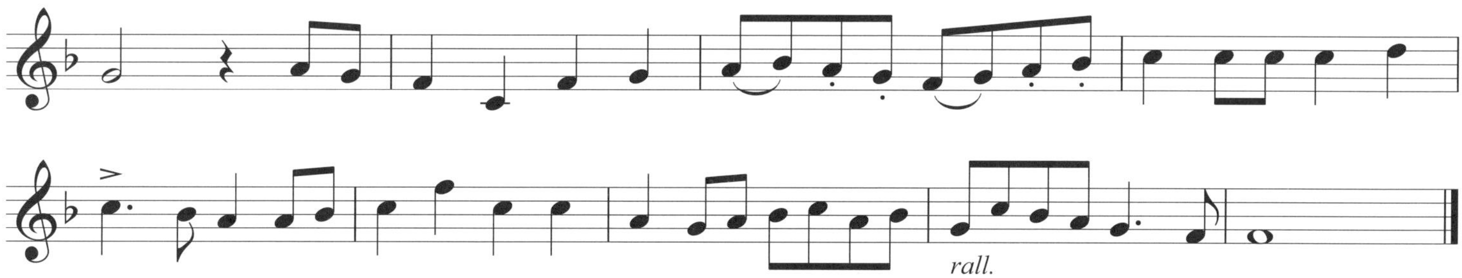

New Time Signature: Cut Time

2 = 2 beats in each measure
2 = half note receives one beat

Cut time is another way to notate 2/2 time and is used more often than 2/2 time. The cut time symbol appears similar to common time; however, the "C" is cut in half.

STARS AND STRIPES FOREVER

By John Philip Sousa

March tempo

f

March Tempo

Modern **march tempo** is 120 beats per minute (BPM). This speed was designed to align with the pace in which a group of soldiers would move together in step (two steps per second). However, some marches associated with various college athletic teams are played much faster, usually in direct proportion to the success on the gridiron or court at a particular point in the game.

New Note: E♭

THE VICTORS (MICHIGAN FIGHT SONG)

By Louis Elbel

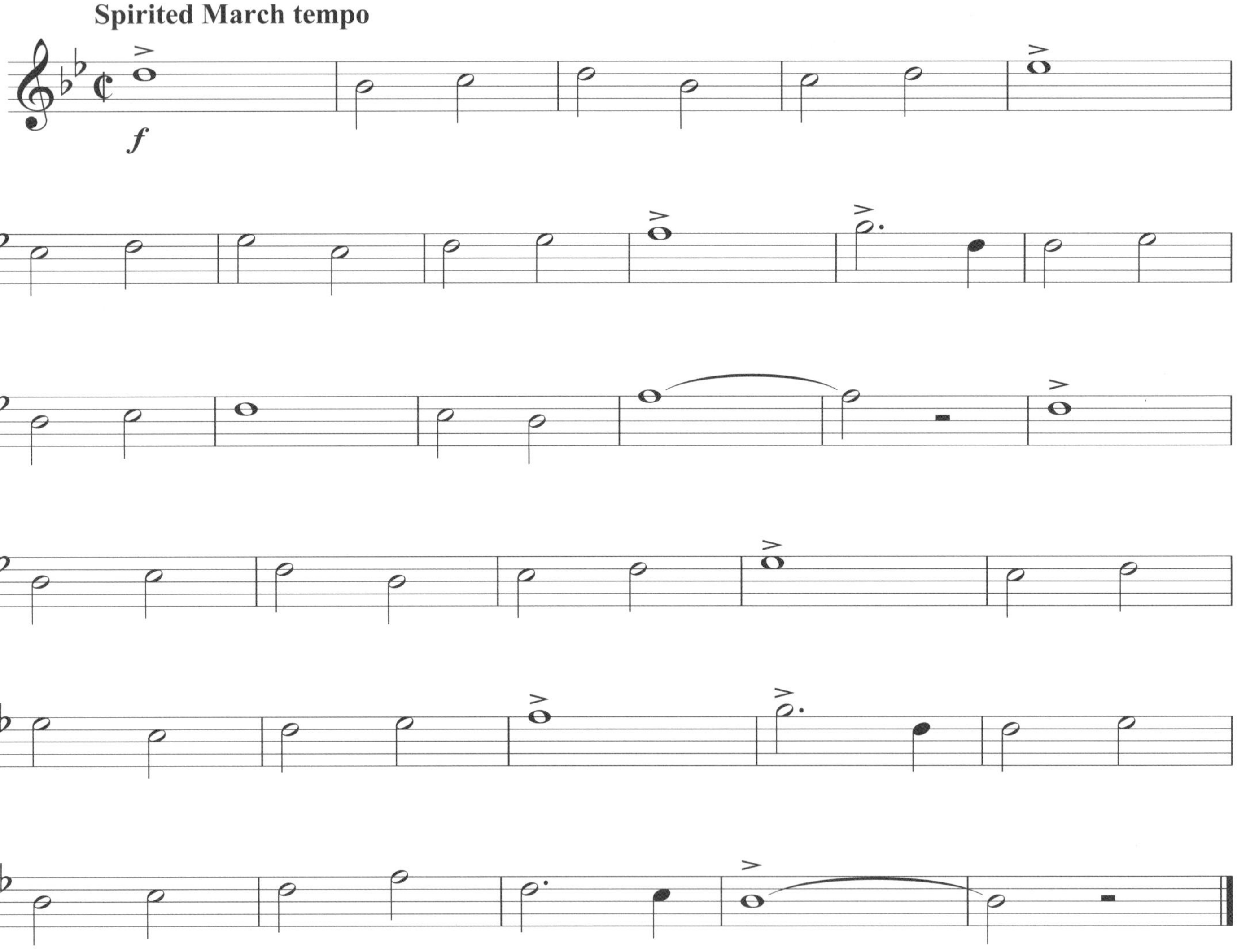

Spirited March tempo

f

Enharmonic Reminder: C♯ = D♭

These two pitches sound the same and have the same fingering.

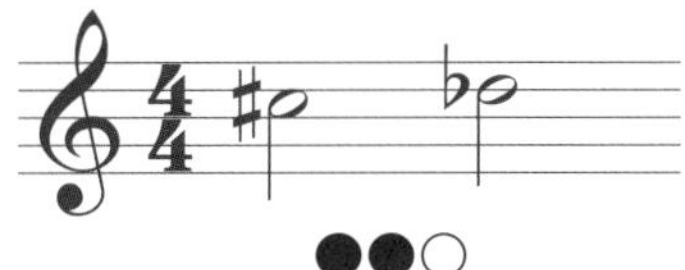

WITCHCRAFT

Music by Cy Coleman • Lyrics by Carolyn Leigh

Swing! (♫ = ♩♪ triplet)

mf

f

mf

TOMORROW

from the Musical Production ANNIE

Lyric by Martin Charnin · Music by Charles Strouse

Trumpet Talk: Practicing and Equipment
Playing a musical instrument is a discipline, much like learning a language or a sport. Daily practice is essential for improvement in both mental and motor skills. One cannot only read about playing the trumpet and do it; it is a skill that must be mastered over months and years to get truly good at it. It is helpful to purchase practice equipment like an instrument stand, practice mute, tuner, and other helpful supplies. If the trumpet is on its stand waiting to be played, you are much more likely to begin a daily practice session.

YOU'VE GOT A FRIEND

Words and Music by Carole King

IMAGINE

Words and Music by John Lennon

Trills

A **trill** is an ornamental device that allows for some interesting effects in music, especially of the Baroque and Classical periods. No doubt you've heard trills being played and wondered how they are done. Although there are a variety of types of trills, depending on the type of music being played, a trill is generally defined as the very rapid playing between two notes next to each other, by moving the valves as fast as possible. Unless specified, all trills should be executed by playing the printed note and the one directly above it in the scale. For example, if the music calls for a trill on a C, and the music is in the key of C, then one would play as quickly as possible between C and D, since D is the next note above C in the C major scale. The trill is played for the written length of the note.

TRUMPET TUNE

By Henry Purcell

TOOLBOX

Toolbox Tip: Dotted-eighth/Sixteenth Subdivision

A common mistake among musicians is not properly subdividing note lengths. One of the most misplayed rhythms is the dotted-eighth sixteenth. This rhythm is often incorrectly played more in the style of the tied jazz triplet, or "swung" eighth notes.

Break a quarter note into four equal subdivided beats. Sing this rhythm in your head and check to make sure the dotted-eighth note is receiving three of the four subdivided beats.

THE STAR-SPANGLED BANNER

Words by Francis Scott Key · Music by John Stafford Smith

FLY ME TO THE MOON (IN OTHER WORDS)

Words and Music by Bart Howard

DO NOTHIN' TILL YOU HEAR FROM ME

Words and Music by Duke Ellington and Bob Russell

Trumpet Talk: Trumpet Pitch Quirks and Tendencies

You may have noticed that your trumpet has a ring on the ring finger of your left hand that can move the third valve slide in and out. Some trumpets also have a "saddle" to adjust the first valve slide while playing. These slides are to adjust tuning on certain quirky notes. The two quirkiest notes on the trumpet are the low D and low D♭. When playing these notes, it is advisable to extend your third valve slide out about a half inch and pull it back in when no longer playing these notes. This is because the trumpet tends to be very sharp (high) when these notes are played. Some players, including the author, find it useful to extend both the third and first valve slide on the low D♭, otherwise the note will sound very out of tune. See page 8 for information about lubricating these slides.

I SWEAR

Words and Music by Frank Myers and Gary Baker

Time Signature/Meter Changes

Occasionally, music changes time signatures, or **meter** throughout the piece. When this occurs, continue counting at the same tempo (unless otherwise indicated), only changing the number of beats in a measure.

ALL YOU NEED IS LOVE

Words and Music by John Lennon and Paul McCartney

D.S. al Coda

When you reach the **D.S. al Coda**, return back to **Del Segno** (the sign) in the music and play until you reach the **To Coda** marking. Jump down to the **Coda** (usually near the end) and play until the end of the song.

Repeat and Fade

Repeat and Fade is a continuous repeat, getting quieter each time. It usually lasts about three or four times.

HEY JUDE

Words and Music by John Lennon and Paul McCartney

Key Signature Changes

Music can change key signatures throughout the piece.

TIME IN A BOTTLE

Words and Music by Jim Croce

Allegro con brio: fast, with spirit

fp: forte piano: play the note loudly, then immediately get quieter

SYMPHONY NO. 5 IN C MINOR, FIRST MOVEMENT EXCERPT

By Ludwig van Beethoven

> **Trumpet Talk: Continuing Your Journey**
> As you near the end of this book, you have developed many skills necessary to perform music. It is now time to take your trumpet journey to the next level! Find community ensembles, chamber groups, jazz combos, rock bands, church groups, or volunteer as a bugler for ceremonies. The best motivation to continue to improve is to find opportunities to showcase your talent.

POMP AND CIRCUMSTANCE

Words by Arthur Benson • Music by Edward Elgar

BUGLE CEREMONIAL CALLS

Trumpet Talk: Bugling
One of the great thrills of being a trumpet player is being asked to participate in a ceremony where you provide the bugle calls. Bugle calls are intended to be played "open" due to the fact that the only brass trumpets available used to be those without valves. Many trumpet players choose to play these calls open, but it may be advantageous to play these with the first valve instead, since it brings these down a step and easier to play in tune.

REVEILLE (WAKE-UP CALL)

Traditional Bugle Call

TAPS (END OF DAY AND TO HONOR THE DEAD)

Traditional Bugle Call

Very slow and reverently - free tempo

TO THE COLORS (RAISING OR LOWERING THE FLAG)

Military Bugle Call

VOCABULARY TERMS

A tempo: return to the original tempo

Accent: an articulation, attack note by playing stronger

Accidental: sharp, flat or natural that appears in a measure

Adagio: slow tempo

Allegro: fast tempo

Andante: slower "walking" tempo

Aperture: the opening that air leaves your mouth and enters the mouthpiece

Articulation: style in which you attack, or tongue each note

Bar line: divides the music staff into measures

Breath mark: indicates where to breathe

Coda: the conclusion

Common time: another way to notate 4/4

Con brio: with spirit

Crescendo: gradually get louder

Cut time: value of each beat from 4/4 is cut in half, also notated as 2/2

Da Capo (D.C.): from the beginning

Decrescendo: gradually get softer

Del Segno (D.S.): from the sign

Dot: adds half of the value of the note

Double bar: indicates new section within music

Dynamics: indicate how loud or soft to play

Embouchure: position of mouth on the mouthpiece

Enharmonic: two notes with the same pitch but written with different note names

Fermata: hold for a longer, unspecified time

Fine: the end

Flat: lowers note a half step

Forte: loud

Fortissimo: very loud

Internal repeat: repeat sign at the beginning of a measure

Interpretation: personal changes made to music with tempo, articulation and dynamics

Interval: distance between notes

Intonation: pitch accuracy

Key signature: indicates whether to play the notes sharp, flat or natural

Largo: very slow tempo

Ledger lines: lines that extend the music staff

Legato: an articulation, smooth and connected

Lip slur: playing more than one note with the same fingering without tonguing

Maestoso: majestically

Marcato: an articulation, "march style" with strong attack followed by decay in sound

Measure: space between two bar lines

Meter: a regular recurring pattern of beats

Metronome: device used to keep steady tempo

Mezzo forte: medium loud

Mezzo piano: medium soft

Moderato: medium tempo

Molto: much, very

Natural: cancels sharps or flats to return note back to its normal state

Octave: interval that is eight notes apart, both notes have the same name

Offbeat: a beat that does not fall on a strong beat

Partials: the individual notes with one fingering

Phrase: musical sentence, or complete idea

Piano: soft

Pickup note: note or group of notes that occur before the first full measure

Rallentando: gradually slow down

Ritardando: gradually slow down

Sharp: raises note a half step

Shuffle: rhythmic feel or groove, first eighth note feels longer than the second

Slur: an articulation, connects two or more notes of any pitch

Staccato: an articulation, light and separated

Staff: lines and spaces where music is written

Subdivision: breaking the beat into smaller, even pieces

Swing: musical style where eighth notes are not even in length

Syncopation: rhythmic change where the emphasis of the beat shifts from the strong beat to the offbeat

Tempo: speed of the music

Tenuto: an articulation, note is held full value

Tie: connects two or more notes of the same pitch together

Time signature: indicates number of beats in a measure as well which type of note receives one beat

Triplet: three notes of equal length grouped together

Vibrato: rapid bending of a pitch

FINGERING CHART

F♯ G♭

G

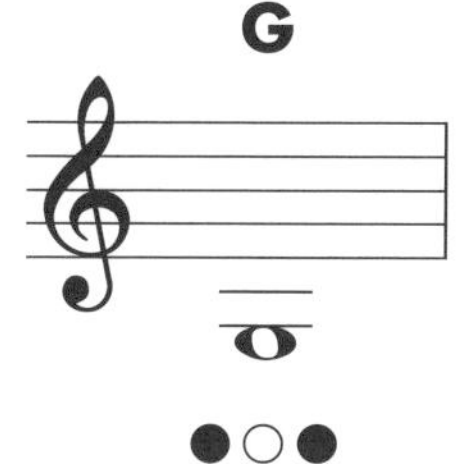

G♯ A♭

A

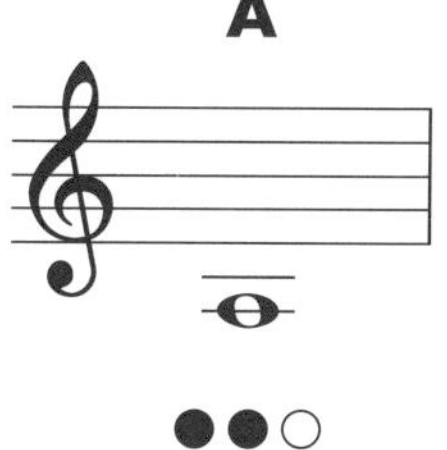

A♯ B♭

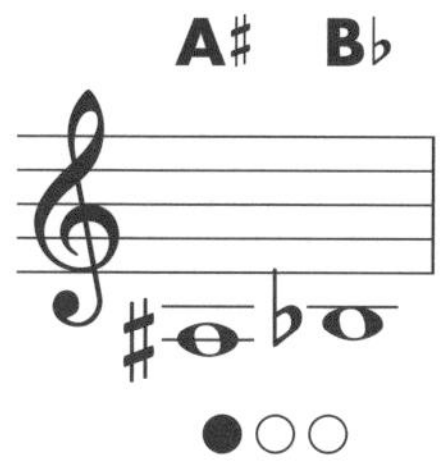

B

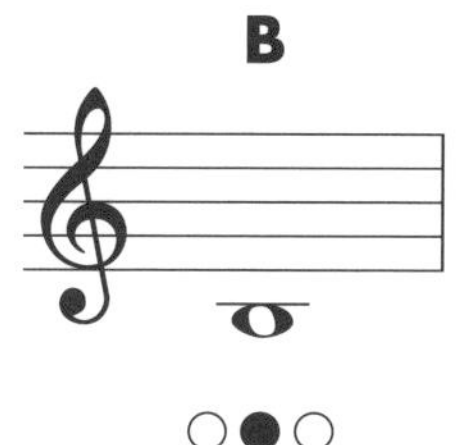

C

C♯ D♭

D

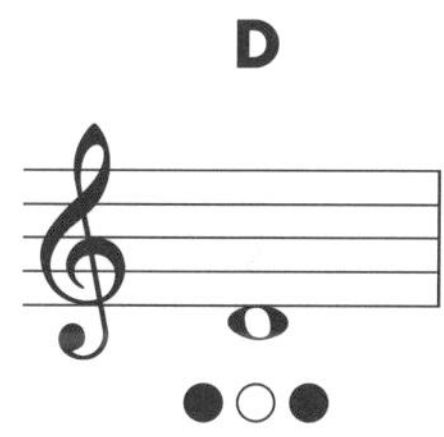

D♯ E♭

E

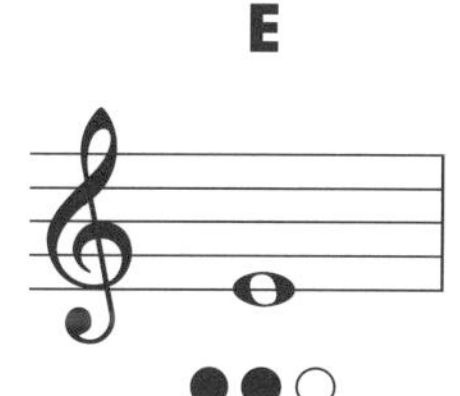

F

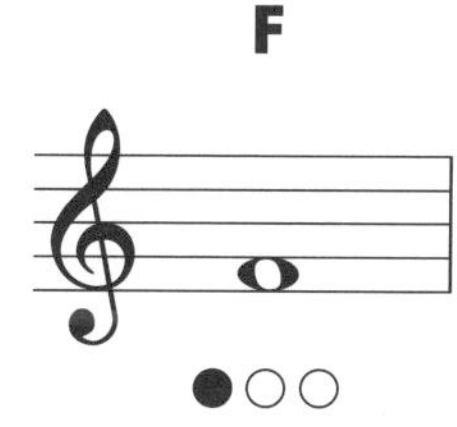

F♯ G♭

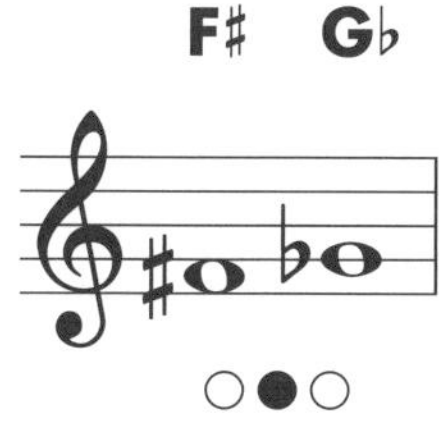

G

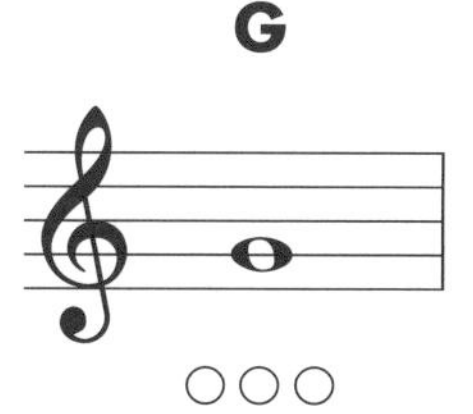

G♯ A♭

A

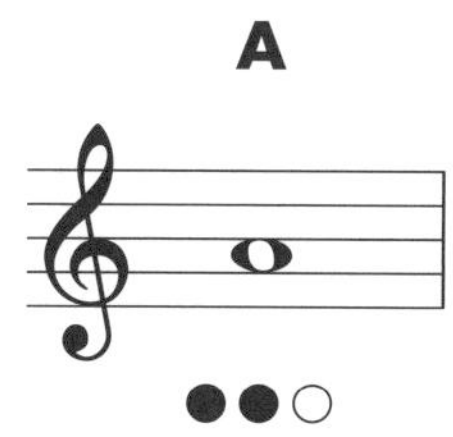

A♯ B♭

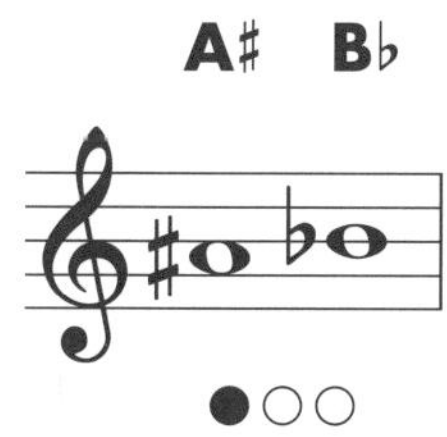

B

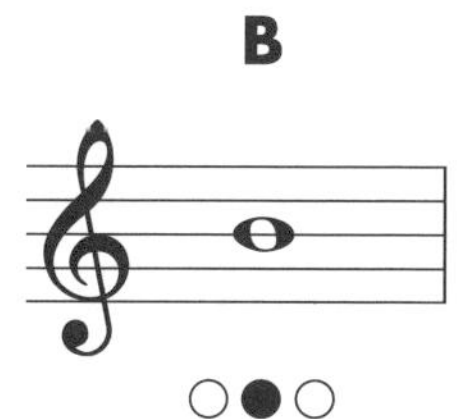

C

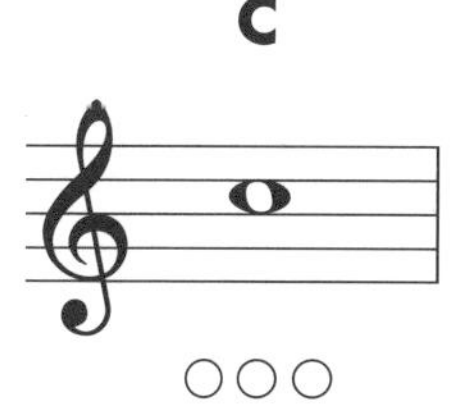

C♯ D♭

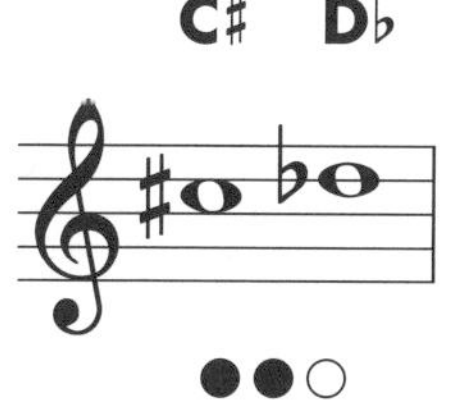

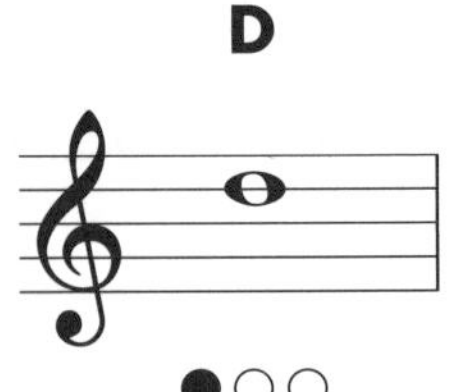
D

D♯ E♭

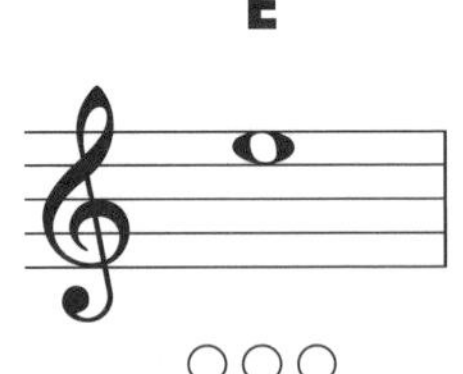
E

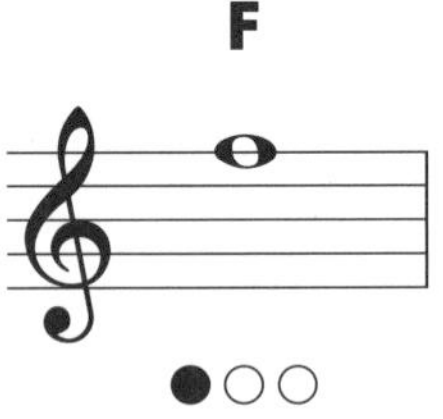
F

F♯ G♭

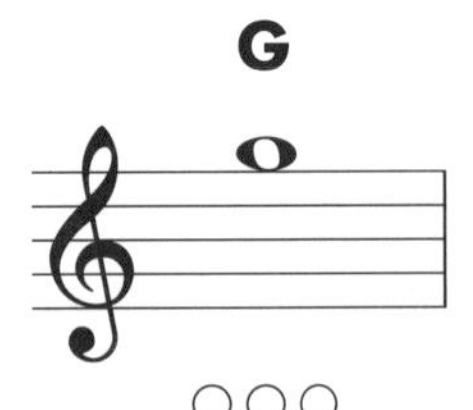
G

G♯ A♭

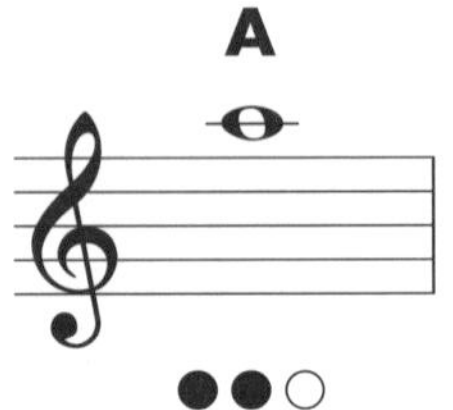
A

A♯ B♭

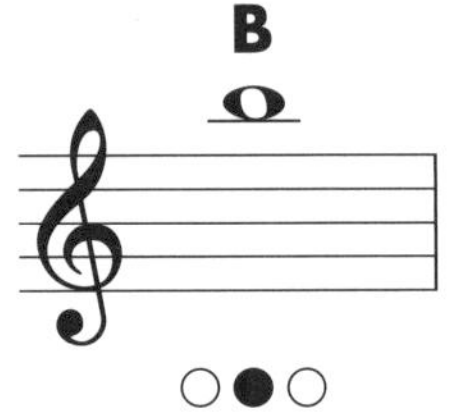
B

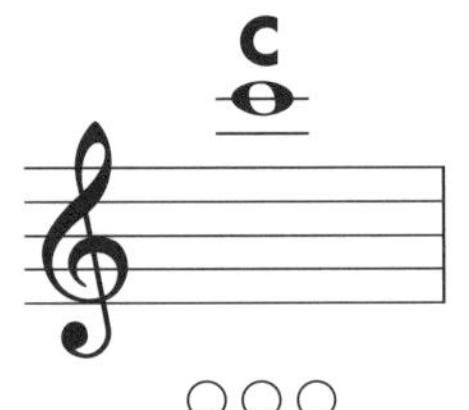
C